Prof. *Deborak*

proftrembla›

MW00974891

No Longer My Constant Bedfellow

Free from the Grip of Domestic Violence

Prof. Deborah A. Tremblay

CROSSBOOKS

CrossBooks™
A Division of LifeWay
1663 Liberty Drive
Bloomington, IN 47403
www.crossbooks.com
Phone: 1-866-879-0502

First published by CrossBooks

ISBN: 978-1-4627-1971-6 (sc)
ISBN: 978-1-4627-1972-3 (e)
ISBN: 978-1-4627-1973-0 (hc)

Library of Congress Control Number: 2012912096

Printed in the United States of America

This book is printed on acid-free paper.

Any people depicted in stock imagery provided by Thinkstock are
models, and such images are being used for illustrative purposes only.

Certain stock imagery © Thinkstock.

rev. date: 07/31/12

I dedicate this book to the *Author and Finisher of Our Faith*, the Lord Jesus Christ. In my Nana's home office, at her typewriter in the late 1970's and early 1980's, in Troy, New York; I frequently imagined I was a writer, and there discovered the existence of His historical burial cloth in *Verdict on the Shroud*, a book by Kenneth Stevenson and Gary Habermas (1981).

Thank You for Your completed work. Even so, come, Lord Jesus.

Contents

Acknowledgment
Concrete Life Lessons

I WOULD LIKE TO ACKNOWLEDGE the role that my great Uncle Jim played in my life. He was my father's uncle, and although the time I spent with him was relatively brief, the lessons he taught me during that time have lasted throughout my life. He died many years ago, yet I've visited him often at 177 Fourth Street in Troy, New York; an address I call upon whenever I have the opportunity to stroll down Memory Lane.

It's there, on Memory Lane that my Uncle Jim's old store, *The Yetts Newsroom*, still stands. In my heart and mind, he and the building that housed his store can never be separated--both stood tall and proud; were strong in structure and sturdy in frame; and both provided shelter for me.

That old two-story brownstone itself told *two stories*—one of a stoic son of Italy who lived above his store, where he provided for an elderly mother who spoke no English; the other of a fatherly man whose strong, quiet love was communicated through the simple experiences we shared. Uncle Jim taught me many life lessons in a language that my child's heart could easily understand.

My parents and I lived directly across the street from him. Their bedroom window looked down upon his store. More than once, my parents punished me for misbehaving by sending me to their room to lie down; instead, I amused myself by jumping up and down upon their bed and observing my reflection in the wall-mirror mounted above their crème-colored veneer dresser. I often toyed with the brass knobs affixed to those six drawers. Most times, however, I'd spy Uncle Jim downstairs outside below, speaking to a friend, and soundly rap upon the window pane, calling,

"Uncle Jim, here I am! Come get me!"

Upon hearing me, he stopped in mid-sentence, glancing upward. He next held up his hand to halt traffic, briskly bolting across the street to my rescue. I remember the crinkles of concern etched into his forehead when he saw me and heard my cry. *I also recall the remorseful expressions on my parents' faces as he scooped me up from their room and carried me across the street to his store!*

Frequently, I ate dinner with my Great Grandmother and Uncle Jim and it was there that I was served *7-Up®* soda—a rare treat in my parents' home. Uncle Jim had never married nor had children of his own, so he lavished his fatherly attention upon me. Over time, his store came to be my, "home away from home." He kept a small stool for me behind the candy counter, near the cash register, where I perched to read comic books, draw, and write.

Over time, I considered that area my own personal space. He kept pencils behind that counter, selling them for a penny each; I regularly snapped, wore down the erasers, and nibbled upon them before returning them to their box. But he never grew angry, just replaced his supply after each of my visits. (Did he see the potential for a writer in me, and recognize that my destruction would have a point?)

Most customers spoke Italian; I understood little. Whenever they'd speak to me, Uncle Jim would bow down and whisper the appropriate Italian responses for me to repeat back. Never would he have let me be an outsider to any conversation. This taught me that I belonged.

I do not condone smoking, yet Uncle Jim occasionally smoked cigars. Beforehand, he'd carefully remove the paper band from around his cigar and slide it over my finger. What a beautiful ring of shiny red and gold foil. To me, those cigar band rings were more precious than any 18-karat gold band could ever be.

Whenever he gave my brother and sisters a comic book and a candy bar, I received *two* comic books and *two* candy bars. That favoritism seemed acceptable--he never deprived my siblings of attention; he just gave me twice as much. These simple gestures made me feel special.

Like Jesus, my uncle was a carpenter. In his workroom, he'd supply me with wood, nails, and a tack hammer so I could work too. He never suggested that girls shouldn't do carpentry. It hammered home to me that I could do anything I chose to, and I've always measured my dreams by *that* yardstick.

Once he carved a toy fishing pole for me and attached a line. I sat on the front step of the store, imagining it was a boat, and pretended to fish on the concrete, my sidewalk sea. Looking back, I realize Uncle Jim's *love* was concrete. Like initials carved into wet cement, his lessons left their impression, solidifying over time.

Today, my imagination grips the store's brass doorknob and squeezes down, unlocking memories. Suddenly, I am a child again, skipping across the slatted wood floor and rushing to my uncle--he is warmth in a wool sweater with leather arm patches; strength in a crisp white shirt and dark trousers; stability in a pair of polished wing tips. He cloaked me in security, vesting me with well-suited lessons that have never faded throughout my life.

The story of my uncle's life was told with his hands. As a boy, he shined shoes to help his family, often earning a man's pay. His parents expected him to study the violin. He favored amateur boxing. When they finally threw in the towel and agreed that he could stop playing the violin after fourteen years, he *never* picked one up again. Instead, he went on to earn numerous boxing belts, medals, and ribbons.

His hands patiently and meticulously crafted furniture. The music of his saw across wood often filled the room. After work, he'd wash his hands in the basin in the back of the store. He used *Lava*® soap; it was strong and gritty, like him. To this day, whenever I smell *Lava*®, feelings of safety and happiness wash over me.

His hands were large, his reach expansive; everyone who knew him felt his touch. His hands were warm; returning the handshakes of countless friends. His hands were gentlemanly; tipping his fedora, holding a door for a lady. His hands were generous, always giving; handing my struggling parents money or an armload of groceries for their four young children. On our walks through the city, he'd offered me his finger to hold. My small fingers encircled it like a glove. It was a perfect fit.

We held hands that way on every walk we took until the day he died. Those hands, now at rest, did their job well. Yet they have never waved goodbye to me. Uncle Jim isn't gone--from the window of *my* heart, he will always be just within view, just across the way, just beyond the door, at 177 Fourth Street, on Memory Lane; waiting for me to call. Thank you, Uncle Jim, for those concrete life lessons and for demonstrating God's fatherly example. I love you.

Introduction

Spring 1985: Far From Free

NIGHT HAS FALLEN; DARK AND ominous. My husband Kirk suspects I intend to leave and knows this will be the last night he will have power; the implications are frightful. The deceptive mask he wore throughout our engagement has fully loosened and fallen away to reveal the true horrors that lie beneath. I recognize an ugly truth: I am in the clutches of a monster. The face of his true agenda all along has been power and control; I see that now. *How could I have been so deceived?*

In retrospect, our relationship was tainted from the start. Tonight, however, it becomes toxic when he terrorizes my young son Joshua; of all of his treacheries, this is the greatest. With my toddler's safety jeopardized and his well-being endangered, I am hyper-vigilant for the first opportunity for Joshua and me to flee. Our escape from harm is the only effective antidote for my failing sanity and broken heart.

During the previous year, Kirk and I stood before the justice-of-the-peace, and with his parents and our friends as witnesses, exchanged civil marriage vows. At this ceremony, he swore to both *love and honor*--a promise that had tarnished as completely as the wedding band he'd placed upon my finger that day. It has become painfully obvious that, in his mind, marriage granted male entitlement, and conferred instead license to both *abuse* and *dishonor*.

When Kirk and I first started dating, I was the single-mother of a young son, Joshua, living at home with my father, Frank, and younger sister, Jill. By way of family history, my parents had separated and divorced when I was seven. I was the oldest of their four children. I lived with my mother until I turned thirteen, when I was then sent to live with my father, shortly after my mother and her new husband gave birth to twins in 1977, a boy and girl whom they named David and Jennifer. My brother Frank, seventeen months younger than me; sister Wendy, three years younger; and, sister Jill, five years younger; continued to live with my mother during the week, and visited my father and me on weekends, where they each took turns staying overnight with us. When I turned sixteen, the Family Court awarded permanent custody of Frank, Wendy, and Jill to my father; and I was suddenly responsible for their care full-time. Wendy would move back into my mother's home not long afterward.

My son Joshua had been born in November 1983 when I was nineteen years old. Pregnant at age eighteen, I had no real relationship with my son's biological father. I did have a spiritual and moral obligation to contact him after Joshua's birth, however, to inform him he had a son, and did, when Joshua turned three months old. I owed this to my baby; it opened the door to a relationship with his father in the future, should my son wish to have one.

Despite the mistakes and misjudgments I had made in my young life, I was Joshua's mother and responsible for his well-being--the time had come for me to acknowledge the poor choice I'd made in marrying Kirk, admit that he had abused Joshua and me, and to forever close the door on this painful aspect of our lives. My only desire was to rescue my son and return us to the shelter of my father's house amidst the safekeeping of my family.

A window of opportunity for Joshua and me to safely leave has been thrown open. Overcome with relief, I realize my husband has gone to visit his parents as he told me he would. I beseech my friend and co-worker, the daughter of the couple with whom we have been staying, to supervise Joshua downstairs while I retrieve his belongings. Escape and survival are uppermost in my heart and mind; I must be quick, and take only what is necessary.

Upstairs, I enter the bedroom. It is very cold. Although numb from pain, I perceive the cold; it permeates through to my bones. Having been physically battered, as well as repeatedly sexually, emotionally, and psychologically attacked by my husband, I have lived in a state of constant distress from the start of our marriage. His deprivations of sleep, food, physical comfort, safety, money, dignity, and freedom have been effective--I can neither hold my head up nor look directly into anyone's eyes. The woman staring vacantly back at me from the mirror is someone I barely recognize; my self-image seems to have long ago shattered. Much like the victim of a "brainwashing" or campaign of terror, I have been systematically isolated from family, friends, and all possible support—the question is: have I been *broken*?

Never have I felt so alone. *Unfortunately, I am not alone at that moment*--my husband has not gone out, but instead hides; concealing himself within a closet, quietly lying in wait. Immediately after I retrieve my suitcase to hurriedly pack, he charges out and ambushes me.

White-hot volts of fear surge throughout my entire nervous system at the sight of him; shockwaves of denial course through my mind and I become limp with fright. Breathless and immobilized, I am at a deadened standstill, stunned that I fell for this deceptive ruse.

"Where do you think *you're* going?" he demands, as he slams the apartment door and engages the heavy metal lock. To my ear, it is the sound of prison bars slamming shut.

"I'll tell you where--you're not going *anywhere*!" he threatens.

My heart beats wildly against my chest wall; while grateful to God that Joshua is safely downstairs, I bitterly regret how foolish I was to attempt to retrieve any of our meager belongings. Frantically, I gather my reason to take in the scene: My husband has hidden most of my clothing; the remainder he has torn to shreds. My jewelry and few valuables I own are gone. The contents of my purse have been destroyed, as well as my contact lenses, which had been soaking in their vials upon the dresser. My appalled reaction pleases him.

In Joshua's room, his possessions are also lost; his winter jacket, shoes, and diapers are missing. These maneuvers, of course, are intended to prevent my leaving. Realizing my error in attempting to salvage our property; I turn and make a desperate bolt for the door.

My husband pursues me, preventing my narrow escape by applying a vice-like grip to my shoulders and wresting my frame. He then whips me around and with one tremendous jolt, smashes me soundly into the nearest wall. I am winded and dazed as my back and skull absorb the impact—the brunt of which leaves a telling impression of the contours of my head in the wall. As plaster fragments fall to the floor, my bones feel as though they, too, have splintered.

As I reel from the effect, he intensifies the assault. Reaching over, he grasps my throat, firmly squeezing until I am in a chokehold. The pressure to my windpipe is agonizing. I can neither yell nor draw breath. As he strangles me, he forces me across the room and down onto the bed. With one iron hand still clamped around my neck, he removes the other, then seizes my bed pillow and presses it hard over my face. Bearing down upon it with all of his might, he simultaneously smothers me. Pinned to the bed, I thrash, kick, and claw at him but cannot free myself. My lungs burn; threatening to burst from suffocation. I lose track of time. How long I have been deprived of oxygen and blood supply to my brain?

Life is reduced to an hourglass he now holds in his maniacal grip; consciousness as well as hope ebb away. *Joshua! My beautiful baby...to never again see your face; hear your laughter; hold you close.... Dear Lord*, I pray from the depths of my despairing heart, *please don't let me die like this; help us escape in Jesus' name.*

All at once, I flood with adrenaline. With one enormous effort, I break free from his hold and take in as much air as possible. While choking and gasping, I swing my legs around the side of the bed, leap upright, and stomp furiously upon the floor as hard as I can to summon help. It is a frenzied dance of fear; at the same time, a terrified scream tears from my soul. Afterward, I double over to catch my breath. *How long have I gone without air?* For a time, I cannot see; eventually the blurring around my field of vision clears. In response to my cry for help, my friends' parents, the Ahrens, have ascended the stairs and are pounding upon the apartment door.

"What's going on up here?" Mr. Ahrens bellows.

"We're...we're just having an argument," Kirk lies, his own breathing labored from the effort he has exerted in his effort to strangle and suffocate me.

"Open up!" Mr. Ahrens orders. "Open this door right now!"

My husband unlocks the door, but not before whispering, "I'll kill you if you tell them."

The Ahrenses storm into the apartment. I am doubled-over, breathless, and wheezing for air. Mrs. Ahrens' hand covers her mouth in disbelief when she examines the hole in the wall having been created by my head.

"What did you *do* to her?" she cries.

"What happened here?" demands Mr. Ahrens.

"He...tried to kill me," is all I can manage. My voice is thin, weak, and strangely unfamiliar.

"You're the one who *married* him!" Mr. Ahrens shouts, thrusting an accusatory finger in my direction. "*What did you expect*?"

Oddly, he requires no accountability from my attacker. At that moment, I am so grateful to be alive and drawing breath that I fail to comprehend this act of victim-blaming, but in retrospect, it's an indictment that has replayed in my memory often over the years.

"Please just let me get Joshua," I beg the couple. "I'll leave your house *right now*; I just want my son." I begin to cry.

Somehow, propelled by an undercurrent of emotion, I make my way downstairs to my toddler. Overwhelmed at the sight of him, I draw him into my arms. Had I suffered another minute or two of oxygen deprivation...I am certain I would have died. What might his future have then been? I push the painful possibilities from my mind as his little arms encircle my throbbing neck.

I carry him to the phone to call my father. As I dial the number, my husband Kirk, who has followed me down to the first floor, tries to convince me to hang up the receiver.

"Don't do this," he manipulates. "If you do, then we can't be together anymore."

I feel I am rushing toward a waterfall of madness, and my mind paddles furiously to keep my reason from capsizing. Cold, clear, reality surfaces; I must remain calm and do what is necessary for my son and me to survive.

I turn my back to Kirk and pray that my father is at home. I don't recall my exact words, but when he answers, I convey that my husband has seriously hurt me and plead to be able to return home. There is anguish in his voice when he tells me to put my husband on the phone.

"My father wants to speak with you," I inform him. Josh and I cling to one another; we are both trembling. I watch and listen in as my husband picks up the telephone extension in the next room.

"I'm not angry at you, *son*," I hear my father claim. Knowing him as well as I do, I easily discern the difficulty with which the term 'son' falls from his lips. Yet at first, I am perplexed by his statement. *How can my father not be angered by what has happened?* It becomes abundantly clear with his next words:

"I just want you to let my daughter and grandson leave. Let them come back to me."

Suddenly, I understand the strategy: my father is appealing to my husband's *sense of power*—permitting him to believe that he still harbors control of the situation—allowing him to, "let" us leave; which, ultimately, may prevent us from further harm. I listen in on my end of the phone as my father negotiates for our safe return; it is as though Joshua and I are being held hostage with our emotions bound and our hands cinched to the back of a chair. I am scared, shaking, and sick with worry.

After hanging up from my father, I phone a cab. When it arrives, I usher Joshua into the backseat and climb in next to him; gladly leaving all else behind. I am twenty-one years old; my son is two. As we drive away, I steal a look in the side view mirror back at the house that has served as much more of a prison than a home during this relationship. That four-digit address becomes emblazoned into my memory.

Ironically, while short in duration, this relationship will proven to have been exceedingly costly—***in ways that will not be possible to calculate for many years to come.*** One of the few memories I have of the days following our return is the look on my sister Jill's face when she remarks,

"Where did those purple handprints around your throat come from?"

Although I may never be able to adequately describe this marriage, suffice it to say, at its heart, fear was my constant bedfellow.

This much is true—I escaped that night, but I was *far* from free.

March 2009
Seized with Fear

I BECOME CONSCIOUS. SOMEONE GENTLY shakes me and calls my name; his voice echoes from the far end of a vast tunnel. My head aches, my limbs are weighted, and only with tremendous effort can I open my eyes or move. Once focused, I see someone who appears vaguely familiar--especially around the eyes--but am at a loss as to his identity.

For a time, I feel disoriented. Eventually, I recognize it's my husband, Matthew, to whom I have been married since 1990; we'd recently celebrated our twentieth anniversary. Glancing at the wall clock in the darkness, I realize I'd fallen asleep on the living room couch overnight and he was attempting to waken me. It is 3:30am.

"Deb, I think you may have had some kind of seizure," Matt tells me.

Mystified and confused, I ponder, *what is a seizure?* I have little memory of our conversation afterward, and no recollection of the "seizure" event he referred to. Later I will learn that, medically, no memory can be formed during a brain seizure.

My sons Caleb, eighteen; Jeremiah, fifteen; Daniel, thirteen, and Jacob, ten; are also present, each having been awakened and appearing stunned. Joshua, twenty-six, is downstairs in his first-floor apartment. Matt sits with me to observe for awhile.

"Do you want me to call 911?" he asks.

When my mind clears, I suggest we wait until morning to decide if I require medical attention. Despite awakening with a shout and experiencing a mild convulsion and degree of confusion, because I am responsive and oriented, Matt reluctantly acquiesces. We determine the best course of action is to visit the emergency room the next day. Should I then need to remain at the hospital, I could be admitted as an in-patient after an examination in the Emergency Department.

The following afternoon, Matt drives me to Albany Memorial, which is an affiliate of Northeast Health, where he has been employed since 1986. He also works on the campus of Samaritan Hospital, another partner of Northeast, where he is Director of Material Handling and Courier Services. (In this capacity, he administered the operation of material handling; storage dispersal; equipment and supplies; courier services transportation; mail; specimens and supplies supporting laboratory outreach; as well as the copier center.) Today, he is Director of the Material Distribution Service Center.

While there, I have blood work drawn, and a cranial computed tomography scan completed. A cranial CT scan utilizes x-rays in order to create cross-sectional images of the head, including the brain. Small detectors inside the scanner measure these x-rays, used to produce individual computerized images, called "slices;" which then are stacked together to form a three-dimensional model of a patient's head. This technology allows analysis of brain injury, infection, swelling, or tumor. No such diagnosis can be made since test results are inconclusive.

My magnesium level is slightly low, but not sufficient to trigger brain seizures. Nothing definitive to explain the seizure can be identified. Because I have never previously suffered a seizure, I am diagnosed with *involuntary movements* by the treating neurologist. Matt and I are instructed to call EMTs should another seizure occur.

The next morning, on March 2nd during sleep, I seize again at 4:00am. We phone an ambulance and I am assessed by paramedics. Declining a second hospital visit, I instead make an appointment with a neurologist in private practice.

Next, I have Magnetic Resonance Imaging, or an MRI, performed, which is a noninvasive procedure that uses a powerful magnetic field, radio frequency pulses, and a computer to produce detailed pictures of the brain, as well as other organs, soft tissues, and body structures. The images are examined on a computer monitor and used to diagnose certain disorders. However, nothing which can explain brain seizures is revealed at that time.

An electroencephalogram (EEG) test is then ordered. An EEG is designed to detect problems in electrical activity within the brain; brain cells communicate with one another by producing tiny electrical impulses. In an EEG, this electrical activity is measured through the use of electrodes attached to and held in place on the scalp. The electrodes are connected by wire to an amplifier and a recording machine; I am sent home with the EEG recorder, whose purpose is to convert the electrical impulses in my brain while I sleep into patterns which will later be viewed and interpreted by a technician on a computer.

Again, no cause for the seizures can ultimately be identified. I am asked several times if I abuse alcohol or drugs. I assure the neurologist that, as a masters-level educated and experienced alcohol and substance abuse counselor myself; I am neither in withdrawal from illicit drugs nor alcohol.

Later that month, to my horror, I seize again during sleep on March 30th at 5:00am; Matt tries to waken me as I lie upon the living-room couch. Once roused, I notice Joshua sitting in our dining room. On a stool in the corner, he resembles a dazed, dumbstruck prizefighter. Staggered under the weight of his worry, he is unaware that I am conscious. I try to call his name; I want to assure him I am fine yet realize this would be disingenuous--I am still very much trapped in twilight.

Each of my other sons likewise wears an expression betraying various levels of terror. Caleb's friend, Cody, who has spent the night, seems panic-stricken. Guilt and shame overwhelm me. Mortified, I realize my clothes are wet; I have lost control of my bladder during this seizure. Slowly, I gather fresh clothes and when better oriented, step into the shower. No amount of soap or hot water is able to wash away my fear.

Following this third seizure, I am again evaluated by the neurologist. Matt is told that EMTs should only be called when I have a seizure lasting more than three minutes, or have two seizures in rapid succession, one after the other. Knowing that the *type* of seizure is most-often diagnosed by the neurologist as he or she assesses the observations of those who witness it, I listen intently but disbelieving to my husband's description of this last seizure:

While asleep, she suddenly emitted a loud moan. Next, she began to convulse uncontrollably; her eyes rolled back into her head; and her legs went up into the air. Her breathing stopped for as long as two minutes. She lost control of her bladder and also lost one of her contact lenses. It took her a long time before she was oriented again—she seemed very confused for awhile.

Based upon Matt's description, the seizures are characterized as *grand mal*, or what has now come to be described as tonic-clonic; meaning they involve the entire brain. This type impairs consciousness and distorts the electrical activity of either the whole or a larger portion of the brain. The seizures are generalized, meaning no specific cause can be identified at this point. Because they only happen during sleep, I am diagnosed with *nocturnal seizure disorder,* and placed on anti-seizure medication.

The zombie-like side-effects of the drugs are severe, and I find I cannot function while taking these medications. Thinking, walking, and even speaking become difficult. I ask my neurologist if he can assure me that I will suffer no further seizures while taking them; he refuses to do that.

I research the topic and learn about the many problems experienced by persons with different types of seizure disorder on various medications, not the least of which are the occurrence of seizures *caused* by medication effects and changes in the medication schedule. Troubled, I gradually discontinue them and try to carry on as before.

In spring, I have a seizure in my sleep on May 15th at 4:46am. During this one, as well as the previous ones in March, Matt observes that I aspirate some of my own saliva--unfortunately, this will become important later.

At some point, I am asked if I have ever experienced a head injury. The neurologist explains that head injuries can result in brain seizures, even decades afterward. Later at home, as I sit at my kitchen table, the Lord brings the domestic violence attack I suffered during my first marriage to my mind.

I am stunned. I hadn't consciously thought about that event for probably twenty years. One night, however, while I slept, one of my sons recounted to me that he heard me cry, "Stop it, Kirk!" during a nightmare I had; on yet another occasion, while one of my son's friends stayed overnight, he also heard me make that same protest during a bad dream.

I research head injuries and realize that the domestic violence assault I suffered back in 1985 could indeed have a relationship to the seizures I experienced in 2009: Not only was my head slammed against a wall, but I was deprived of oxygen and blood supply for a long period of time due to suffocation and strangulation. I learn that such oxygen deprivation can itself *cause* what is termed *anoxic or post-hypoxic seizures.*

Equally troubling, I begin to have petit mal seizures-- momentary events while awake *where I speak to others not present*, or suddenly *speak with lack of awareness to those who are present;* I refer to these events as, 'blips.' I cannot recall these petite mal seizures, just as I lack recollection of the grand mal seizures. No memories are able to be formed during a brain seizure--this is the reason I never have any memory of these events; it also confirms that the 'blips' I suffered were indeed a type of mini-seizure. Sadly, were it not for Matt and my sons providing me with vital details, I would have no information about them at all.

I continue to work. As a professor of criminal justice at a local community college as well as an online instructor for three state universities, I teach several on-campus and online classes per day. My work attendance is good and I am able to substantially perform my duties as I always have.

However, once during class, a student appears taken aback by something I have stated during my lecture.

"*What?*" he laughs, as he flips quizzically throughout his textbook.

As though in the midst of a daydream, I suddenly returned to reality, yet have no recollection of what I may have said or done. I went on to teach my lecture as I always have. Again, because no memory can be formed during a seizure, I am completely unaware of what may have occurred during that moment. Looking back upon that experience today, I can only reason that it may have been a type of mini-seizure. Of course, I never realized at the time what had happened—*the irony of not being able to form a memory is that you cannot recall what it is that you do not remember.*

On another occasion, I am driving with my son Caleb when he suddenly states, "You just 'blipped'." He tells me that while stopped at a red light, I looked up, pointed, and gushed, "Look—look at the light," in a dreamy voice. I have no memory of this moment and, understandably, am deeply distressed over it.

From that point forward, I determine I can no longer drive my car--although I safely drove us to our destination without incident, I realize I must now be driven to work. Neurologists indicate it is safe to drive only after several months of having no such events. On average, I experience three or four such episodes per month, generally in the evening, of which I am aware.

Over summer, I seize during sleep on June 18th at 5:36am and have two separate seizures on July 22nd; these at 8:00am and at 3:30pm, the latter as I sleep due to the effects of the former; afterward, I am utterly exhausted. Following a seizure, it takes time to recover from the clouded thinking; throbbing headache; intense jarring sensation in the pit of my stomach; and muscle soreness due to the convulsions. When I seize, I also frequently draw blood as I bite my tongue or scratch my face. Nonetheless, physical recovery is straightforward—as a rule, I spend the next twenty-four hours after a grand mal seizure asleep.

Eventually, however, *I am alarmed to find that my short-term memory has been impacted by the seizures themselves.* Unable to recall significant happenings within the last several years, I battle with depression. *Ironically, I am able to recall events from forty years ago much more readily than events from just four years ago.* This leads me to wonder: Can I rely upon Matt and my sons to help me piece together the past?

I search my college email account, which contains thousands of messages in its *Inbox* and Sent *folders*, to help jumpstart my memory. *As I peruse the contents, I experience an unfamiliar sense of detachment; as though reading another woman's personal communications.* A vague guilt gnaws at me: Have I violated another's space and privacy?

Over the course of the summer, I gradually begin to lose energy. It occurs so slowly that I barely notice the changes. My stamina decreases. I have trouble sleeping and cannot negotiate stairs as well. It takes me longer to arrive at my classes, and I have difficulty lecturing for 50 minutes; previously, an effortless task.

On Sept. 10th, I seize at 2:00am during sleep. I feel ashamed, humiliated, and embarrassed, as though I am failing everyone, and wracked with guilt over putting Matt and my sons through more terror. No one, however, is more terrified than me.

I develop persistent cold-flu symptoms and cannot breathe well. This further interferes with my rest, and sleep-disruption increases the risks for additional seizures. On September 19th, I seize twice while asleep, once at 12:00am and again at 5:30am. Unable to keep up with its demands, I resign from a Thursday evening teaching job I have recently landed.

My primary care physician refers me to a cardio-pulmonologist. After several tests, I am diagnosed with *empyema*, which is an accumulation of pus in a body cavity such as the chest, caused by aspiration pneumonia. In my case, the infection is attached to the outside of my right lung, in the pleural cavity, causing pressure and pain. My lung capacity has been severely reduced; it is as though I am smothering. The goal of treatment is to cure the infection and remove the collection of pus from the lung. As to the cause, I am told it occurred as a result of the aspiration of my saliva during several of the previous seizures I have experienced. This has resulted in a pneumonia which cannot be treated solely by antibiotics; lung surgery will be necessary.

A procedure called *decortification* must be performed. Because my right lung is no longer able to expand properly, the surgeon will need to peel away the lining of the lung. A chest tube will be inserted to completely drain pus that subsequently forms and antibiotics will be used to control the infection. On October 27th, the surgeon operates for over five hours. Under anesthesia, an incision is made in my upper back, my right lung is inflated, and the infection painstakingly removed. After spending ten days recovering in the hospital, I am discharged.

I recover at home for six weeks under the *Family and Medical Leave Act (FMLA)*. On January 1st, after not having any brain seizures for a period of three months, I again seize at 4:00am while asleep. During this seizure, I fall to the floor and strike my eye. I am the recipient of a black eye for the next two weeks. Each time I look into the mirror, I feel shame.

As the start of the new term approaches, the prospect of returning to work greatly concerns me. With the twelve brain seizures I have had over the course of the past year, I've experienced short-term memory loss. How will this affect my teaching? Will I have difficulty retrieving or conveying information during one of my lectures? Worse still, what if I were to experience a 'blip' while in the classroom? How will I know what has happened and how do I handle such an event, should it occur? Will my return to full-time on-campus teaching somehow *cause* a seizure?

Various scenarios play out in my mind, each as frightening as the other. I long to speak to someone about these fears, but don't want to further upset my family. Can my husband understand how helpless and inadequate I feel? Am I able to properly parent my sons? From a human standpoint, even with the support of family and several friends, I am very much alone.

I return to class on January 19, the first day of the spring 2010 term. Colleagues and students welcome me back, and I feel very strong! My teaching? As effortless as it ever was. It appears my fears may have been unfounded.

However, on January 26th, I have a 'blip' at 7:30pm while sitting on my living room couch. My husband tells me I utter silly things and poke him in his stomach. I've learned from experience that a 'blip' is a prelude to a seizure; each time I have 'blipped,' I have seized one week later. Like clockwork, on February 2nd, I suffer two seizures; one at 2:00am and another at 5:30am.

This necessitates my calling in sick on February 3rd. I seize again during sleep overnight on February 3rd at 12:10am, but feel I must nonetheless attend work the next day. It is a concerted effort for me to teach the morning after this seizure--in the midst of a thick fog, my short-term memory is severely clouded; I have trouble with tasks like word retrieval, ordinarily one of my strong suits. Bereft of the tools of my trade; I am literally at a loss for words.

Is my future in jeopardy? What about my life? Several teaching colleagues who are closer than others inquire about my health and are astonished to discover that the seizures have recurred.

"You're *still* having them?" one professor remarks. Her tone is dismissive. "You were having them *last* year." She eyes me with mild disapproval; as though I were a student turning in a late paper rather than a colleague describing a life-threatening seizure disorder, who would be only too happy to never have one again.

Family members draw clear battle lines. I am pressured into going back on medication; accused of not helping myself; deeply criticized; and somberly judged. I wage war with depression, anger, confusion, shame, guilt, and fear. The assault I experienced in 1985 plays itself over and over in my mind.

After more than seven years of teaching criminal justice courses at Hudson Valley Community College (HVCC), I resign my position over an unrelated contract issue; concluding that I cannot fight both battles well. I continue to teach distance learning courses at home via my laptop for several other colleges and also seek additional opportunities to expand my teaching credentials. I must still help to support my family, regardless of the neurological nightmares with which I grapple.

In between instructing college students online and homeschooling my three youngest children (in grades six, eight, and ten), I determine to become an expert on the topic of seizure disorder; specifically, *post-traumatic epilepsy*, which refers to recurrent seizures following a traumatic brain injury—in my case, <u>with an epileptogenesis</u>

of twenty-four years between the injury and the first seizure.

This is the story of how I became free from the grip of domestic violence *twice* as a result of my first marriage--the first time I physically escaped him in 1985; and the second time I emotionally and psychologically escaped his clutches in 2010--a full twenty-one years after his death.

Chapter One:
Glimpses Into the Futuristic Keyhole

IN JANUARY 1985, I MADE my way to the new CVS store in the atrium in downtown Troy, New York, to inquire whether there were any job openings. I was given an application by the clerk, and carefully filled it out, neatly penning my recent retail experience as a temporary cashier at two local college bookstores. I detailed my previous work history; at sixteen, I'd worked in a florist shop and at eighteen, a diner, so I possessed adequate experience to land a part-time job in the new store, should the manager require personnel. He politely accepted my application, although he indicated at that time that the store had no available openings. I thanked him for his time, noted that his name tag read, *Matt*, and wished him a good day.

Over the previous couple of months, I'd taken two temporary retail positions through an employment agency, one at Hudson Valley Community College's *Vikings Cove Bookstore*; the other at Russell Sage College's bookstore. I tried not to envy the students who perused the store aisles as they searched for various texts and supplies yet admittedly it was difficult--they had the privilege of attending college classes, something I felt I could only fantasize about as the twenty-year old single mother of a one-year-old son.

Nonetheless, these jobs during the "college rush" of returning students in the fall provided an opportunity for me to sharpen my cashiering and sales skills, while also allowing me to earn income toward the purchase of diapers and other baby supplies. Since my son Joshua and I lived with my own father and my youngest sister, Jill, our basic needs were provided for, but I had begun taking steps toward self-sufficiency and self-betterment; I wanted my son to have a mother of whom he could be proud.

Unfortunately, due to emotional and psychological issues in my past, I had dropped out of high school at age sixteen. I had given birth to my son when I was nineteen. When he turned six-months old, I enrolled in a program to earn my GED (General High School Equivalency Diploma). After completing the curriculum, I returned to my old school, Troy High School on Burdett Avenue, and sat for the examination. I was delighted to learn that I had set a record in my state, having earned a nearly perfect score during that sitting. Looking back in my life, there have been many such situations in which the Lord has given me that kind of victory over my former personal failings. If I can take credit for anything, it is for providing Him with ample opportunities in which to do so.

While at home one day with Joshua, I received a telephone call from that CVS manager, Matt Tremblay, in which he explained that a part-time cashier position had become available, and requested that I come in for an interview. The following Monday, I arranged for my sister to babysit Joshua, and rode the public bus into downtown Troy. At the mall, I requested that the manager be paged. As I waited for him to come downstairs from his office to the sales floor, I glanced around the store. When he appeared, he held my application, and asked me to follow him to his office.

In the office, we reviewed my qualifications, experience, and interest in the job. He described the job duties, company policies, store procedures, and thanked me for the interview. On my way out, I briefly chatted with a friend from high school, Dina, who had recently begun working there. I told her I hoped to soon be her co-worker, and headed outside to catch the bus home.

The following day, I received a call from that manager in which he offered me the position. I would work a part-time shift from either 9am-3pm or 12pm-3pm, for a total of 21 hours per week. Since my sister Jill agreed to watch Joshua for me, he could stay comfortably at home while I worked. In this way, I could gain a bit more work experience and Jill and I could both bring in additional income. My father made a good living as a numismatist, but Jill and I each had our own personal expenses with which to be concerned. The extra income would help purchase clothes, diapers, and food for Joshua.

The following week, my cashier training began. Fortunately, my previous experiences working the college rushes paid off well; in no time at all I was quite comfortable behind the counter. Jill often brought Joshua downtown to me in his stroller at the end of my shift; from there we would often go shopping or meet friends. My sister was very responsible and took great care of my son.

Over time, I was promoted to key personnel. Now part of the management team, I functioned as head cashier. It was my job to supervise the other clerks, provide cash for their tills, count down their cash drawers, and prepare the daily bank deposits. I also resolved problems with customers as well as in the store pharmacy. Eventually I was asked to open and close the store during various shifts. Soon afterward, I was promoted again and offered the position of store closer.

During this time, I began developing personal feelings for Matt. The more that we worked together, the more interested in him I became. He had many good qualities and seemed to be genuine and kind. However, although religious, I knew that he was not a Spirit-filled believer. I told myself that, for this reason, I was being unwise.

You're also a young single mother with a toddler, I reminded myself. *Matt isn't going to be interested in the 'package deal.'* Still, I turned the idea over in my mind and wondered, *Is it just my imagination, or does he care about me too?* Over the course of that year, he and I spent a great deal of time together on the job; we often spoke in the office as we prepared paperwork.

One Sunday dinner at my grandmother's home, she told me that she and her friend often sat at the water fountain in the atrium and watched me work in the store. She placed her hand over mine.

"That young man *likes* you," she insisted, referring to Matt. "Nana, how do you know that?" I asked, rather taken aback. She smiled. "I've seen the way he *looks* at you."

That previous December, at a prayer meeting I attended every Friday evening in a town called Schaghticoke, there were several prayers for me by the congregation. Among others, was a prayer that the Lord would, "give me a companion—one who would understand." At that moment, when members of the fellowship laid hands on me and prayed, a heavy burden had lifted from my heart.

One day, while I worked in the greeting card department, Matt came over to ask a question. He lingered there, and it appeared as though he wished to discuss something, but perhaps had thought better of it. Reluctantly, he'd walked away. All at once, I heard the Lord speak to my heart:

I will put a love in his heart for you.

I was speechless yet certain I had felt those words in my heart in a way that was impossible for me to have conjured myself. A few days later, at about the same time, I was restocking greeting cards when the very same thing happened. Matt approached to ask a question. It seemed as though he intended to discuss an issue with me but reconsidered, and, once again, headed away toward his office. A second time, I felt the Lord speak to me:

Even now, I am speaking to his heart.

THERE SEEMED TO BE NO denying it this time. At that moment, a quiet sense of peace enveloped me.

One day as I tended the cash drawers of two cashiers at the front register, Matt entered the checkout area, carrying overstock items from the back storeroom in white plastic bags, which he planned to display on shelves and pegs behind the counter. These items, such as cigarettes, film, and other high mark-up products, are considered high-risk for shoplifting.

As Matt approached the checkout, set several bags upon the floor, and stooped over to begin restocking the items, the Lord allowed me to have a foreshadowing of the future. I received an unmistakable glimpse of a time to come when Matt and I would be working together in another context putting groceries away. *Several years ago, in our kitchen, Matt stooped to retrieve groceries that he had just brought in from the car in small white plastic bags. As he did, I re-experienced that very same moment.*

On another occasion, one of our co-workers out on maternity leave brought her newborn son in for everyone to see. *As she held him out for us to view, carefully cradling his head, I observed Matt as he looked down at the baby and had another such experience in which I came to know that he and I together would both be holding a newborn at some future date.*

I believe the Lord allowed me these glimpses into the futuristic keyhole for two reasons: First, to glorify Himself and secondly, to build my faith and assure me that as the Alpha and Omega, He knew the end from the beginning and *He held the key*; all I had to do was believe and trust Him to bring His Will to pass. *Unfortunately, something was to occur during this period of time that would not only cause me to doubt my understanding of the Lord's revelation, but ultimately bring consequences of severe harm to both myself and my son.*

What I am about to describe will be unsettling. In fact, if someone were to have predicted that the events I am about to disclose could have ever happened to me and my son Joshua; I would never have believed it. In retrospect, I may never know for certain *why* the following events occurred, nor *how* I got into the position I did in the latter half of 1985. What I am about to describe to you is painful, shameful, and in some respects, horrifying to revisit, but *it must be told*. Suffice it to say, were it not for the diary I kept for my son Joshua back during this time (in a journal purchased from the first bookstore in which I worked the college rush), I would have been unable to piece these events together or put them into their proper context. Therein lays both my task and challenge: My sharing this story may well prevent other young women from suffering the same fate that I did; I pray that every woman who reads these words will ultimately learn from my mistakes.

You see, as it would happen, rather than trust the Lord and wait on Him to open the door to a relationship with Matt *in His time*, I became increasingly impatient over the course of those months, and began trying to strong-arm the door to Matt's heart. When I did this, I stepped out of the Lord's will, stopped trusting Him, and gave the enemy a foothold in my life.

One day while Matt and I were in the office, I simply wasn't willing to wait any longer. As we sat there, I foolishly decided to take matters into my own hands and unwisely ventured forward despite my awareness that he did not at that time have a personal relationship with the Lord.

"Matt, I have something I want to tell you," I began.

"What is it?" he light-heartedly replied as he continued to prepare paperwork, without turning around to face me.

"Well, it's...*personal*," I explained, hoping he would glean the nature of what I hoped to divulge.

"Personal in what way?" he responded. "Is something wrong?"

"Well, I wanted you to know that...uh...I...I *care* about you," I confessed.

Immediately, the atmosphere in the room had changed; the air between us became charged with tension.

He had a difficult time turning around to face me.

"When you say...that you *care* about me," he finally answered, "how do you mean that?"

He tentatively met my eyes. I didn't stop to consider my next words before I spoke them; I only thought of my own personal needs and desires and of how lonely I was.

"I mean that I have...feelings for you that are...*beyond the workplace*," I emphasized.

He was silent for a short time. "CVS frowns on personal relationships in the workplace," he announced, "especially between a manager and an employee...but, I don't...I don't think it will be a problem. It's not...it's not like I would be taking you out after work or anything." A minute or two of awkward silence ensued.

"I think that's all I wanted to say," I told him. "It was just beginning to interfere with my work, so I thought I'd get if off of my chest."

"Well, I'm glad you told me;" he smiled, "now it's out in the open."

Just then, a cashier paged the office, needing assistance with a customer. I gladly grabbed my keys and went downstairs to assist, trying to push the incident from my mind. I was mortified.

What were you thinking? I chided myself.

Unfortunately, not only had my loneliness clouded my judgment in this instance, it also made me more vulnerable and subject to victimizing by men in general. It is commonly understood that an abuser "hand selects" his victim; seeking out particular traits or characteristics that make this woman a better candidate in his mind for such victimization.

Please don't misunderstand: *in no way am I suggesting that women who ultimately are victimized by men deserve, desire, or have "asked" for such ill-treatment. What I do suggest, and what the social-scientific research literature on domestic violence supports, is that men who abuse women enter the relationship with the specific agenda to exercise power over their partners and therefore choose women whom they believe, for whatever reason, would be easiest to control.*

One evening, an acquaintance named Kirk I'd briefly met several years earlier at a friend's house reintroduced himself to me at a diner while I was out with Joshua. As I stood in line about to order, Kirk maneuvered around the front of my baby stroller, eyed my son, and without a word, handed me a key ring with a framed photograph of an infant attached. I examined the picture of the male baby, then politely handed it back.

"Is he yours?" I asked.

He nodded affirmatively and smiled.

"This is Joshua," I indicated, referring to my baby. "What's *your* son's name?" I inquired.

"Kirk Anthony," he proudly boasted, "after me. He lives with his mother."

I didn't know it at the time, but <u>this assertion had been his very first lie to me</u>. Kirk had no son. *I wouldn't learn until much later in the future that his key ring picture was, in fact, a <u>baby picture of himself</u>--Kirk carried it around with him everywhere he went.*

Chapter Two:
The Most Dangerous Time

IN THE MEANTIME, MATT WOULD transfer out to another CVS store. At that location for a short time, he decided he no longer wished to work for the company and resigned. After he had left CVS's employ, he would occasionally visit me at our old store. Kirk and I had been frequently seeing one another by then. Over the course of that year, my relationship with Kirk had become more intense. Unfortunately, in spite of the many warning signs I received regarding Kirk's anger and possessiveness, I was blinded to these dangers by several factors; not the least of which was my damaged self-esteem. In short, I had simply come to believe that Matt was, "too good" for me; consequently, Kirk was, "the best I could do."

During the first of these visits, Matt had learned of my engagement and impending marriage to Kirk. When I'd told Matt, he'd cavalierly remarked, "Well, when it's right, you know it, I guess." On a subsequent visit, we stood in the greeting card department conversing as I worked to replenish the stock. As I reordered wedding cards, Matt steered the conversation around toward my own wedding plans.

"So," he ventured after a long, uncomfortable pause, "when's the *big day*?"

"We're already married," I'd brusquely informed him. "We had a small civil ceremony on November 2nd."

He wore a look of disbelief until he spied my wedding band. He then took several awkward steps backward. I noticed that the color had drained from his face; he appeared ashen.

Serves you right, I silently thought. *That'll teach you to play with my heart.*

I turned to Kirk then, who had just entered the store and come up alongside us where he had found Matt and me speaking.

"Matt left CVS," I explained to Kirk, "He no longer works for the chain."

My husband turned toward Matt, who continued to look bewildered by the news. Kirk, instantly taken aback, wore a look of mock disbelief. *"You?"* he smiled, with a feigned familiarity that somehow set off alarm bells within my subconscious mind. To any outsider, it would appear as though Matt and my husband were the closest of friends, yet Kirk barely knew him, having only fleetingly spoken to him once or twice before. Something about the sophistry of that gesture greatly concerned me on some deeper level, which, at that moment, I couldn't put my finger on.

Prior to my engagement to Kirk, the Lord Himself had attempted to warn me. While at work one day, I made my way down the main aisle toward the back of the store to respond to a clerk's call for assistance. As I did, I thought about Kirk and Matt, pondering which of these men the Lord would have in Mind for me as a husband and for Joshua as a stepfather. The Lord had *clearly* communicated and revealed His Will to me concerning Matt being, 'the companion who would understand,' yet I tried to convince myself that because Kirk claimed to be a believer, doled his attention upon Joshua, as well as attended church services, that it indeed *had to be* Kirk.

All at once, I felt the Lord begin to chastise me. From the top of my head to the bottom of my feet, I began to spiritually smart all over, as any child might after a physical spanking. My Heavenly Father unequivocally required me to obey Him and follow in his revealed Will; He was displeased with my reasoning yet was lovingly and patiently correcting me. The sensation persisted. Finally, I told myself that *Matt* could not possibly be the Lord's intended choice as a husband for me--at the heart of my anger toward Matt was what I had come to believe was his stinging rejection of me.

What I would soon learn was quite the contrary—in fact, it was *Kirk* who had not been the proper choice and my decision to marry him despite my knowledge it was against the Lord's revealed Will would have severe consequences for both me and my son.

During this time, Joshua and I continued to attend church services whenever we could. Kirk often attended with us. At two of these particular meetings, I received prophetic messages through another believer. These precious words from the Lord have never failed to sustain me; aside from engraving them onto silver pendants several years ago, I have them etched deeply into my heart.

The first came at a ladies' meeting I attended one Saturday; other believers in the Lord prayed for me at that gathering. As they did, the Lord clearly spoke through one of them. I heard Him state:

Deborah, you have been named after someone mighty in the Lord; you are like a torch and you will be a light.

The second came at a meeting I regularly attended at Friday night fellowship. There, the Lord spoke through another believer:

Fear not, for I have anointed you to be a witness as you have dreamed of. Be bold in your confession.

On some level, I came to understand I had married Kirk to spite Matt. Once Kirk and I married, it didn't take long for me to realize the magnitude of the mistake I had made. First, he began to exert ever-increasing control over various aspects of my life. It began with my appearance: He started a subtle campaign for me to no longer wear makeup, to cut my long hair, and to substitute eyeglasses for my contact lenses. Next, he claimed that his mother felt very uncomfortable by the style of clothing that I wore—he suggested I wear jeans and tee-shirts so she would feel, "less intimidated" by me. I resisted the pressure he exerted upon me in all of these areas, *yet failed to recognize them for the efforts at power and control that they represented.*

He criticized the few friends I had, accused my co-workers of wanting to date me, and made it increasingly difficult for me to get ready for work in the morning. He started to sabotage my job: preventing me from leaving for work on time, insisting I take days off on a whim, calling me numerous times during the day, showing up frequently at CVS while I was on shift, and watching me from the mall as I worked. He himself lost one job after the other.

He began behaving in ways which upset my new store manager, Vern, as well as my family, friends from work and church, the Ahrenses, my babysitter, and anyone else with whom I could have a relationship, allegiance, or alliance. What might have been his agenda? Could it be to make my world as small as possible, until there was nothing left in it but *him*?

One evening I asked my friend Heather to keep an eye on Joshua then went out for a brief walk after dinner. When I returned home, Kirk was outraged.

"Where have you been?" he roared.

"I went for a walk, that's all," I explained.

"Who with?" he demanded to know.

"By myself," I assured him.

He shook with fury. "I thought someone kidnapped you and threw you in their car!" he insisted, as he threw the Ahrenses' items angrily around their kitchen.

"DON'T EVER DO THAT AGAIN!" he shouted.

As a foolish young person, I mistook this display of power and control as a sign of love and concern. It was anything but.

On another occasion, I had gone to my grandmother's home, located several short blocks away. Joshua had been asleep, and it had been a cold winter night, so I gave him a kiss and tucked him safely into in his bed. When he nodded off, I jotted Kirk a quick note so that he would know where I was, hoping that would placate him. While at my grandmother's home, the phone rang and I answered it. Kirk was on the line, ordering me to return to the apartment immediately. He was furious that I had left.

"I'm going to take Josh out of his bed, put him in the stroller, and take him out in the cold," he threatened. "You know what else? I'm not going to put his winter coat on him or even a dry diaper."

"Kirk, no," I quietly begged him, "please don't do that. Don't take Josh outside. It's too cold. I'll be back right away; I'm leaving now."

I kissed my grandmother goodbye, and tried not to alarm her as I hurriedly left. My heart pounded as I raced back to the apartment. Halfway there, Kirk came around the corner pushing Josh in the stroller. When Josh saw me, he burst into tears. Thankfully, he was wearing a jacket and was dressed warmly. I grabbed the stroller and made sure he was alright. I then ensured that his blanket was tucked in all around him, and pushed the stroller as rapidly as I could back toward the apartment.

When I saw my baby burst into tears, deep down inside, that's when I finally knew that I *had to leave*. The following day, I would begin looking for our next available opportunity—*this is the time that domestic violence expert Dr. Lenore Walker refers to as, "the most dangerous time" in an abusive relationship.*

That next morning, Kirk told me he planned to visit his mother and stepfather. I decided that this was my chance to escape; when he left, I would gather my few belongings, take Joshua, and leave. I didn't know if my father would permit me to return back home, but I believed he would help Joshua and me once he understood the situation. I felt so ashamed of myself for having been deceived but for the sake of my son, I would swallow my pride, humble myself, and ask my father if we could return home.

I didn't see Kirk anywhere, so I knew he must have gone to visit his parents as he said he would. I told my friend Heather, the Ahrens' daughter, that I planned to take Joshua and leave.

"Would you please watch Josh for me?" I beseeched her. "I need to go upstairs to pack our things and get out of here before Kirk gets back."

She nodded. "Josh can stay downstairs with me until you are ready to go."

"I'll be quick," I told her. I gave Josh a peck on the cheek and a reassuring smile. I didn't know it at the time, but **that would be the last time my son would see me whole.**

Upstairs, as I opened the door to the walk-in closet to retrieve my suitcase, *Kirk immediately charged out from his hiding place in that closet and ambushed me….* Over the course of the next few moments, my life would change forever.

Time seemed to slow down as he grabbed me, and sent me reeling into the wall. I found myself on the bed, dazed and in a chokehold, being strangled and fighting for my life. As the pillow came down over my face, I was certain I had breathed my last. **That would be the day I was attacked, strangled, and suffocated in the bedroom— and the night a ticking time-bomb was planted within my brain—but wouldn't explode for another twenty-four years.**

Chapter Three:
Clearly By Design

Back when I was a teenager, I had taken a part-time job in South Troy, in a florist shop owned by my second cousins. They had been in business for many years and designed fresh, silk, and dried floral arrangements for a living. During the time I worked there, they trained me, and I learned basic floral design, care and handling of fresh and artificial flowers, customer service, and basic shop operation. The knowledge would serve me well in the future.

It was while I was originally employed there at age sixteen in 1980 that my grandfather, whom the family always affectionately called *Pop*, passed away. I helped work on his funeral flowers at the time, which were designed in the shop's backroom then delivered on to the funeral home. Later, the arrangements would be transported to the cemetery for all to view. I found that assisting in the designing of his funeral flowers proved to be an effective way to deal with many aspects of my grief. Eventually, I would leave my part-time job there and go on to other types of employ. In the future, however, quite unexpectedly, I would return to that very same shop to design when it came under new ownership.

Fast forwarding years ahead to 1988, I again landed a job there when the shop was about to change hands to a new owner, Phyllis Prezio, who would purchase the business from my aging cousins, then open a second store location in another part of town, which would house both a fresh flower shop as well as a craft store. I was twenty-four years old at the time and working at the new shop when I received an urgent phone call from Matt. At that point, he and I had been dating steadily for two years and our relationship had become serious. Joshua was five years old at that time.

"Deb! Have you...heard?" Matt asked, sounding a bit out of breath.

"Heard *what,* Matt?" I was somewhat distracted at first since I had been preparing to close up the shop.

I sensed him grappling for words. At that point, I suddenly became concerned. "Is Josh alright?" I pressed him.

"Yes, he's fine. This is...about *Kirk,*" he emphasized.

I paused for a moment. The name always caused me to shudder. *I will not be afraid of him,* I determined. Our divorce had only recently been finalized, but not after several issues had to first be addressed by the attorney we had hired.

"What *about* him?" I questioned in exasperation. *What problem could he possibly be causing for us now?*

Several seconds passed.

Matt's words echoed like the bang of a judge's gavel: "He... he was just *killed.*"

My breath caught. I experienced a deep and profound sense of finality, as when a court's judgment is handed down or jury verdict rendered.

"Huh? What are you *talking* about?" was all I could summon.

"I just heard it on the news," Matt told me. "Apparently he had car trouble out on the highway and went to get help. When he tried to cross the street, he appeared to get caught in the glare of an oncoming car's headlights...and... was struck down instantly. He died at the scene."

I stood there, stunned. I relived the night he had strangled and suffocated me and how I had nearly breathed my last. My hand found my throat. Knowing the abuse and terror he had perpetrated upon Joshua and me, my heart pounded. I shuddered again. I was no longer afraid of Kirk--suddenly I was afraid *for* Kirk.

It would be months later, while still employed at the new florist shop the second time around, that my grandmother, whom the family all lovingly called *Nana*, passed away. Just as I had worked on Pop's funeral flowers, I subsequently worked on Nana's.

I find it noteworthy that I had just begun working in that florist in May of 1980 when Pop died one month later in June; likewise, I had shortly been rehired at that same shop the second time around in November of 1988 when Nana died one month later, in December. Working on her funeral flowers at that time was also very therapeutic for me, just as it had been the first time around when my grandfather died. Nana and I had always been closer than any grandmother and granddaughter; perhaps even as close as any mother and daughter could be.

As 1989 then turned to 1990, Matt and I set the date for our wedding at September 22nd and began working toward that goal. We decided on the church, met with the pastor, and booked the reception hall. We chose *Mario's Restaurant*, which was previously owned by my Nana's sister back when it was known as *The Airport Inn*. In my mind, it was the only place to hold our celebration in order to pay her tribute.

Just as I had learned a great deal about the fresh flower business from my cousins, I would also go on to become quite skillful in silk and dried arranging from my new employer. Over the course of my employ there, she taught me well and I would go on to create and design all the silk flowers for my own wedding, including the bouquets, boutonnieres, and centerpieces, as well as fashion the designer bows for the church and reception hall. (Seven-year-old Joshua was our ring bearer and accompanied us on our honeymoon.)

I continued to design for others until I was ready to open my own cottage industry from my home, which I named *The Joshua Tree of Crafts & Floral Design*. Over the next five years, I would go on to book many weddings, host numerous floral and craft parties, as well as teach several craft classes at Hudson Valley Community College (HVCC) in Troy.

Matt and I also began to build our family. Joshua would be followed by younger brothers: Caleb, Jeremiah, Daniel, and Jacob. Caleb was born in July 1991; then Jeremiah would arrive in March of 1994. Back in January 1994, we had purchased a two-story home after outgrowing the apartment we had previously rented.

Like many others, I became riveted by the OJ Simpson trial in 1995. I grew intensely interested in the criminal law at that time; and particularly in issues of domestic violence. When the televised Simpson verdict was handed down, for me, it was as though time stood still. I rose from my seat and uttered five words I had never before dared to articulate. It was as though a proclamation had emanated from somewhere deep within—it was a divine appointment of sorts.

"I'm going to law school," I vowed.

In order to make this possible, the Lord lead me to open a registered family day care in our home in 1995; this provided additional income for our growing family as I pursued my education. Daniel would be born in April of 1996. In fall of 1997, after learning what credentials were necessary in order to qualify for admission to Albany Law School in Albany, New York, I applied to Hudson Valley Community College (HVCC) as a part-time evening student in the college's criminal justice program. I would need to first earn an associate's degree there; followed by a bachelor's degree at a private four-year institution.

One of my current associates, Kathleen Cogan, clearly recounts the evening I first walked into her criminal law class in fall of 1998 as an HVCC student and spoke to her after class.

"I just wanted you to be aware that I am expecting a baby at the end of the term," I had informed her. "My due date is around Christmas time."

She eyed my midriff politely, smiled, and nodded. *I had no way of knowing that, years later, she and I would be teaching colleagues together in that very department.* Jacob was born at the end of that term in December of 1998, not long after final exams.

During my studies there, on a number of occasions, as I learned more about domestic violence, criminal victimization, and crime statistics, I agonized over what Joshua's life might have become had I not survived the assault I had suffered back when he was a baby. In retrospect, I had to ask--who would have properly raised, cared for, and loved Joshua in my absence? What might his future have ultimately been?

I also couldn't help but contemplate that my four younger sons would never have come to be. In the midst of each anniversary, birthday, holiday, or special family event that Matt and I celebrated with our five children; with every gift we opened or candle we blew out, that silent specter loomed, hovering in the doorway, ever lingering at my elbow.

I continued to operate my home-based daycare during the day and attend classes in the fall, spring, and summer evenings. I learned about financial aid that was available to me, and discovered I qualified for full state and federal assistance.

One night after class, I entered the campus computer lab. I knew nothing about using a PC; in fact, as I signed in on the student log, surveyed the room, and noted the fifty or so computers that filled the lab, I would receive what would be my first impromptu computer lesson. As I sat down at one of the PCs, a lab monitor approached.

"Would you...could you....show me how to turn this thing on?" I had tentatively asked him.

From then on, twice a week after each of my 3-hour classes, I walked over to that computer lab while waiting for the arrival of public transportation to take me home and taught myself how to conduct electronic research. Eventually, I became proficient in how to navigate the *Internet*.

One night while surfing the Internet in that lab, I came across the Web site for the *Shroud of Turin* at http://www.shroud.com/menu.htm and perused its contents. There I uncovered forensic information that supported the authenticity of the burial shroud of Jesus Christ; *the same cloth I had learned about in my Nana's home office in the paperback book*, Verdict on the Shroud. I was amazed to see the Shroud analyzed by the latest forensic technology and astonished that more people did not know about His burial cloth.

With my financial aid refund, and after purchasing my text books, I bought a PC for my home; a luxury we never could have otherwise afforded at that time. I was then able to take computer classes as electives for credit in my degree program; I would next go on to take several of my undergraduate criminal justice courses online via distance learning. Today, after earning both of my master's degrees online and teaching a number of synchronous as well as asynchronous distance learning classes over the past ten years, I would confidently match my computer skills against just about anyone's, except, of course, those of my own sons.

After graduating with honors from Hudson Valley Community College (HVCC) with my associate's degree in December 2000, I then transferred to the Sage Colleges in Albany, applying to their criminal justice bachelor's degree program. Sage is a quality private school in consortium with Albany Law School. I reasoned that credentials from Sage might make me a more attractive candidate to Albany Law.

Over time, I was able to close my daycare and begin working at the Sage Colleges bookstore in downtown Troy, (formerly the Russell Sage College Bookstore where I had temped as a cashier in the past); they had relocated to a new facility close by to the Troy campus and I was hired there as weekend manager to operate the store and supervise the staff. The bookstore catered to Russell Sage College faculty, Sage students, and the general public. We sold text and trade books, college supplies; and offered other academic-related services to customers. It was also my responsibility to promote the store's criminal justice, law, psychology, and sociology sections; to do this, I chose selections and read many titles in order to knowledgeably assist our customers. I assisted with author book-signings, special projects, and campus events while pursuing my own criminal justice degree at Sage Albany full-time during the evening.

One evening in particular, I had the pleasure of meeting Dr. Michael Baden, world-renowned forensic pathologist, medical examiner, and author; who came to campus to promote his most recent book, *Dead Reckoning: The New Science of Catching Killers*. In this work, Dr. Baden and his co-author, Marion Roach, discuss the contamination of vital forensic evidence that occurred at the Nicole Brown Simpson/Ronald Goldman crime scene in Los Angeles in 1994 as police and lab personnel allegedly failed to follow basic protocol in the gathering of that evidence. The acquittal of OJ Simpson for these homicides continued to weigh heavily on my mind--*had a grave injustice occurred in this case? Had domestic violence ultimately lead to murder? Would the truth concerning these deaths ever be known?* These questions challenged much of what I thought I knew about our justice system.

I would next face a challenge of another sort: In order to attend classes on the campus of Sage Albany, located next to the Albany Law campus on New Scotland Avenue, I confronted one of my greatest personal fears when, at age 36, it became necessary for me to learn to drive. Neither of my parents had ever possessed a driver's license, nor had either ever owned a vehicle during their brief marriage to one another. Although it might seem mystifying to some, due to a car accident I had once gotten into, I was fearful of ever getting behind the wheel myself. However, with the Lord's empowerment, I confronted that fear. I started off slowly, acquiring and studying a driver's manual; obtaining a learner's permit; then taking a number of professional driving lessons. Over time, I went on to earn my driver's license.

Afterward, I'd practiced the drive zealously from home to Sage Albany and back again; both during the day and in the evening and in all types of weather and road conditions. When the start of classes arrived, I was then able to easily drive myself to and from school. That semester, I attended college full-time in the evenings; transferring my two-year degree from HVCC into Sage under the terms of an articulation agreement. Two years later, I graduated with honors and a bachelor's degree in Criminal Justice Policy in 2003. I was then able to resign my weekend position and set my sights on Albany Law School of Union University in Albany, NY.

Chapter Four:
For Such a Time As This

UNFORTUNATELY, THE FIRST TIME I applied for admission to Albany Law School of Union University, I was not accepted. Upon opening and reading the university's rejection letter, I was stunned—*I was certain that the Lord had called me into a law ministry and had given me the intense desire to attend in the first place.* I could not understand the precise reason I had been rejected—my academic credentials were certainly as competitive as those of my peers.

At first, blinded by that disappointment, I failed to see His Hand at work, but in retrospect, his purposes would become crystal clear. In the interim, He would lead me to go on to earn two master's degrees online from Nova Southeastern University (NSU) in Ft. Lauderdale, Florida; the first in criminal justice, and the second in mental health counseling.

It was while earning both of these degrees studying part-time there that I would meet and study under Dr. Lenore E. Walker (The Battered Woman, 1979), creator of battered women's syndrome; learned helplessness; and the cycle theory of violence. You see, it was not only there that I would work on a domestic violence case with Dr. Walker; it was there that I would better come to understand the Lord's plans and purposes for my life.

Undaunted, and perhaps even *more* determined than ever, I continued to dream of going to law school and of advocating for victims. In December 2003, I served as an immigration caseworker for the *International Center of the Capital Region* (ICCR) in Albany, New York, where I interviewed and counseled clients who were in pursuit of family-sponsored immigration petitions; lawful permanent residence status; and naturalization and citizenship benefits.

In July 2004, I audited a 15-week *US Asylum & Immigration Law* course at Albany Law School of Union University, while still working on my MS in Mental Health Counseling through Nova Southeastern University (NSU) in Ft. Lauderdale, Florida. Concurrently, I enrolled in Dr. Walker's *Introduction to Domestic Violence* class via distance learning through NSU, and at once recognized the pivotal role that this world-renowned domestic violence expert, author, lecturer, and educator could play in providing the necessary expert opinion evidence that Professor Leech required on behalf of his domestic violence client in order to prevail in his case.

His client, a battered Costa Rican mother and her two young sons, sought to petition the American courts for asylum through the *Greater Upstate Legal Project (GULP)* of NY on domestic violence grounds under the *Violence Against Women Act* (VAWA); a somewhat newer area of the asylum law. VAWA, a federal law passed in 1994, was developed together with professionals from the private bar, prosecutor's offices, victims' services, the courts, and law enforcement. It began as a grassroots effort in the early 1990's to urge Congress to adopt legislation to address domestic violence. Today, VAWA also protects against dating violence, stalking, and sexual assault by providing training, education, and funding services that protect child, teen, and adult victims from these crimes by a coordinated response through community-based organizations that exist at the state and local levels.

Dr. Walker, professor at the NSU Center for Psychological Studies from which I would go on to graduate, is also a member of the faculty of the *Institute for Trauma and Victimization* at NSU as well as the Executive Director of the *Domestic Violence Institute* (www.dviworld.org), a not-for-profit organization dedicated to education, research, and public policy issues surrounding domestic violence. Dr. Walker has a national practice in forensic psychology and often testifies on issues of psychological impact and interpersonal violence/trauma; including domestic violence and violence against women.

I would go on to assist the course instructor, attorney Seth Leech, and lawyers with the *Greater Upstate Legal Project* (GULP) by serving as volunteer law researcher and case assistant on their domestic violence-based asylum case out of Costa Rica. Happily, I was *indeed* able to persuade Dr. Walker to donate her time on the case and to provide her services and written testimony in support of our client's petition, *free of charge*. The following communication is an excerpt from emails I exchanged with her on 3/9/2010:

Dear Dr. Walker,

I hope that you remember me. In 2004, I was your distance-learning student at Nova Southeastern University and we worked together on a domestic-violence based asylum case from Costa Rica in which you provided expert opinion testimony on behalf of a young DV victim for a local immigration attorney with the Greater Upstate Law Project (GULP) of New York, during the time that I was simultaneously auditing a 15-week US Asylum &

Immigration Law course at Albany Law School in Albany, NY.

I earned two master's degrees at Nova and also went into the field of teaching; I have taught criminal justice, psychology, sociology, and addictions courses both on campus and online at various colleges and am currently on leave from Albany Law School, where I am a JD candidate.

I am compiling a book on the topic of my experiences with domestic violence. During my first marriage in 1985, I was assaulted the night I tried to leave the relationship (the most dangerous time, of course) and was suffocated, strangled, and had my head slammed into a wall. I was deprived of oxygen for a long period of time. Eventually, I escaped by crying out to my Creator to free me but wasn't aware that I sustained a brain injury that night. The epileptogenesis on this injury was 24 years, but last year, in March of 2009 (21 years after my first husband's death), I began occasionally experiencing anoxic or post-hypoxic brain seizures during sleep as a result. I am researching post-traumatic brain injury and post-traumatic epilepsy; my goal is to write a book over this next year that will take a different perspective on this topic and warn young women about this disorder. How I wish I had known about these types of injury and insult back in 1985. I am emailing to send my regards and also to ask your permission to discuss having been in your class at Nova, your work on the GULP project, and your cyclical model of domestic violence in my own work. Would that be acceptable to you? Please advise. Thank you very much.

Best Regards,
--Deborah A. Tremblay
Isaiah 9:7

Prof. Deborah A. Tremblay

Dear Deborah,

The book you are writing is very necessary. There are many forms of closed head injury that we see in formerly battered women as they age especially from shaking and head banging—much like 'punch drunk boxer's syndrome'. Often women become involved in a minor car accident that wouldn't have caused much damage and then cannot recover from it because it sets off the deterioration process. We don't know a lot about the actual brain processes but it surely does exist. Yes, of course you may use whatever work that you wish of mine.

Warm regards,
--Lenore Walker

In a subsequent email message to a detective friend of mine on 3/25/2010, I explained to him how Dr. Walker came to be involved in the GULP case I had worked on:

Mike,

I was cross-registered in her class at NSU and in my Immigration class at Albany Law when I volunteered to work on the case with my law professor. I didn't know the case was an asylum case on DV grounds at our first volunteer meeting. When I learned the grounds for the petition, I told the group that I believed I could convince Dr. Walker to donate her time on our case. They were all non-plussed; not realizing who she was.

At the following meeting, my law professor was on top of the world. He obviously had done his research. He walked into the law class, threw up his hands and exclaimed, "Do you have *any idea* who Debbie's law professor *is*?" When we won, I was so gratified that this former victim and her two sons were awarded asylum. Mike, if I hadn't been there, Lenore Walker would never have been involved and there is a good chance the courts would not have granted this young woman's petition for asylum.

--Deb

Today, GULP is known as the *Empire Justice Center* (http://www.empirejustice.org/) and works on a broad range of legal issues, including domestic violence as well as child care, civil rights, disability, housing, health care, immigration, and public benefits matters.

I am deeply grateful that I could work with Dr. Walker in obtaining American citizenship for that Costa Rican spousal abuse survivor and her two sons under the provisions of VAWA. There is little doubt that our client's application for asylum was granted by the immigration court based upon Dr. Walker's expert testimony.

In addition, *__had I been accepted to law school the first time I had applied, I never would have pursued either of my masters' degrees nor studied with Dr. Lenore Walker.__* I never would have met her nor ever have been in a position to approach her to request she donate her time and testimony on the asylum case on which I had been volunteering. In retrospect, it is quite obvious to me that the Lord had placed me in that position--despite the many mistakes I have made in my life--for such a time as this.

Chapter Five:
From Criminal to Therapeutic Justice

OVER THE YEARS, I HAVE also had the privilege of working in several other capacities as the Lord has opened doors of opportunity to me. Please allow me to share these with you.

In 2002, He lead me to become a Certified Sexual Assault Counselor and Advocate through the *Volunteer Sexual Assault and Crime Victims Assistance Program* (SACVAP) of Rensselaer County in Troy, New York. For the five years that I volunteered with SACVAP, I maintained my certification through the *New York State Department of Health (NYSDOH)* by satisfying the appropriate in-service and continuing education requirements and working several 12-hour shifts per month. During my assigned shift, I wore a pager and when a client phoned the hotline number, the hospital paged me so that I could call in and be connected to the crisis caller. As a certified sexual assault counselor and advocate with a local hospital, I provided advocacy, counseling, and crisis intervention to callers of 24-hour hot line; hospital/medical escort and police station accompaniment to victims of rape, sexual assault, and domestic violence; and offered referrals, outreach, and education to those victimized.

After earning my master's degrees, the Lord then put me in a position to provide group therapy to mentally-ill, chemically addicted (MICA) clients of a day-treatment program, in which I delivered individual and group counseling sessions; facilitated groups; and designed treatment programs in accordance with regulations of the *NYS Office of Alcohol and Substance Abuses Services* (OASAS). I was able to serve as a community residence counselor there and supervise 18 female residents of the halfway house OASAS operated. During that time, I also provided counseling and crisis intervention while facilitating a Women's Group twice weekly--educating clients on issues of domestic violence, sexual abuse, and the justice system. Collaborating with House staff and the House Manager, I also resolved disputes; diffused conflict; and build trust and rapport among our program's participants.

The Lord then lead me to serve as an outreach worker for a homeless agency in which I operated a van and distributed food, clothing, and blankets to homeless men and women on the street. My team and I performed needs assessments for the homeless population in Albany as well as tenants of the program's single room occupancy residential building. We provided referrals for service and transported these clients to area detoxification centers, shelters, and hospitals. My team and I provided advocacy; crisis intervention; and referred men and women for necessary follow-up services. We also developed rapport and built trust with the intoxicated, substance abusers, the mentally ill, and the general homeless population. We responded to phone calls from local citizens and numerous human service agencies. Frequently, we also interacted with Albany Police and Emergency Medical Services. Our clients were men and women with significant histories of homelessness, criminality, mental disorder, chronic alcoholism, or drug abuse. We also counseled and referred victims of domestic violence.

Not long afterward, I was hired as a civilian police matron for my local county jail to supervise female arrestees detained in police custody pending their arraignment before the judge. My responsibilities included assessing this population for signs of distress or suicidal risk; performing pat downs; conducting cell checks; and preparing legal documentation according to the policies and procedures of NYS law. In this capacity, I was able to provide crisis intervention and emotional support to a diverse group of young women, including substance abusers and recidivist offenders; and found that most had past histories of chemical or alcohol addiction, mental illness, sexual abuse, and domestic violence. I realized that these were hurting women, like me.

What did the Lord show me through these experiences? I have seen with my own eyes that victims of abuse themselves often suffer and repeat the cycle of abuse and violence *within their own lives*. It is perhaps one of the greatest injustices we see in this vicious cycle of sin and one of the reasons I most desire to advocate for victims of abuse in the future.

Over the years, in both my work and my studies, the Lord has also opened my eyes to the problem of *police-perpetrated domestic violence*. This is something many people loathe to talk about or to even acknowledge. Just as it sounds, police-perpetrated domestic violence refers to battering incidents that occur within the police family *at the hands of law enforcement officers themselves*—those sworn to uphold the very laws they themselves come to violate. Why might this happen?

Some have pointed to a, "police personality" as an explanation. As I teach my students, there is no recognized, 'police personality' in the social-scientific literature, primarily because studies done within the police organization have been quite limited. What is the reason for this? We have understood for some time that the police society *itself* is secretive if not insular, and traits such as fierce loyalty and silence have come to be highly valued among our officers. There is also a high degree of isolation in police culture. Over the years, many officers have come to believe that only other sworn law enforcement officers are capable of understanding the nature of the work they do, and the unique pressures they face. This tends to increase their deep sense of cynicism or skepticism toward others. These factors have made studying officers on the job to be challenging if not outright impossible.

What about policing *style*? It was James Q. Wilson (1968), who first developed the concept of *policing styles* among law enforcement officers; specifically, the *watchman*; *legalistic*; and *service* styles. While many may take issue with Wilson's classic study *today*, might his findings shed some light on our understanding of the unique police culture?

According to Wilson, officers who utilize the watchman style of policing primarily are concerned with order maintenance and tend to judge the seriousness of legal infractions by how the law views them rather than by the immediate and personal consequences they create. Officers who identify with the legalistic style of policing will utilize formal police mechanisms in a given situation, by making an arrest or urging a citizen to file a complaint, rather than by solving problems through the use of available informal solutions. Officers who adopt the service style of policing see their chief responsibility as protecting the public order, whether that calls for law enforcement *or* order maintenance, intervening in situations frequently but with little formality.

Regardless of style, police are called upon to handle a wide range of situations with often-limited training and expertise. In approaching such situations, the "crime fighting" role of officers may not be effective in the community, when officers are called upon to serve in their capacity as "public servants" or "social agents." This is particularly true with regard to issues involving non-criminal family disputes, interpersonal conflict, mental disorder, suicidality, chemical addiction, or social problems such as homelessness. Yet police are called upon daily to intervene in such situations.

Frequently referred to as the "gatekeepers" of the criminal justice system, police also play a critical role in areas of social control. In addition to the legal system, they are involved in the social service; mental hygiene; healthcare; and political systems as well.

According to the American Bar Association (1980), police fulfill several important functions within the criminal justice system. Following arrest, they formally charge suspects with misdemeanors or felonies; detain and interrogate criminal suspects; question witnesses; secure and process crime scenes; conduct criminal investigations; conduct surveillance; notify and interview crime victim's families; conduct identification line-ups for crime victims and eyewitnesses to crime; testify as witnesses against criminal defendants in court proceedings and at trial; and perform many administrative tasks.

Within these functions, police authority is broad, unquestioned, and in certain instances, may be unchecked. In carrying out their responsibilities over time, officers eventually develop specialized skill sets and aptitudes that enable them to maintain two essential tools of the policing trade: *power* and *control*. Officers also have enormous *discretion*, or decision-making ability, in deciding how to use such power. The decision to arrest, or to intervene in some other way, may depend upon whether the task before them involves law enforcement or order maintenance. In either case, the *demeanor* of the individual with whom the officer interacts may determine whether he takes that party into custody or uses some other official show of authority or force during those exchanges. Reaction to that stance of police *power and control* may largely determine the degree of force ultimately used against that person. Once having been internalized by law enforcement officers, might this very process become a *conditioned response* in his pattern of relating to others, perhaps spilling over into vital interpersonal and family relationships?

Because police departments have embodied the bureaucratic form of organization since the turn of the century, they have often been rigid, inflexible organizations, unable to adapt to change. Consequently, police departments have often failed to respond to changes in patterns of crime, and to the composition of the local communities they have served. In true bureaucratic style, police departments have frequently become self-serving, isolated organizations insulated from the true needs of the public. Problem solving within such a structure is rarely designed to deal with root causation. Instead, it is quantified by tracking such indicators as police response times, arrest figures, and crime clearance rates. As a result, officers, as rank-and-file members of the police organization, might find themselves applying the same, tired, short-term solutions to complex, long-term problems in which they are not rewarded for insightful analysis of social problems nor taught to mediate or arbitrate between parties to resolve interpersonal issues. *Such skills are not ordinarily valued in the policing organization.*

Again, police are recognized and rewarded mainly for tasks associated with enforcement and displays of *power* and *control*. Police officers are *conditioned* to respond to others in this manner; it is precisely from just such a stance that officers derive their *legitimacy* in the eyes of members of the public with whom they interact. Displays of power and control are *legitimizing* to the extent that they expected, recognized, accepted, and complied with by others--*officers are rewarded for such displays.*

Bureaucracy itself stifles individual creativity--a quality often valued and even prized in the private organization. Over time, one noteworthy byproduct of this process has been observed in the form of *lowered officer morale.* Serious officer morale problems have been linked to lack of opportunity for personal fulfillment in police work and little chance for career advancement within the formal police organization. At what cost? Low morale has been associated with officer "burn-out;" which in turn has contributed to increasing levels of alcohol and substance abuse, brutality, corruption, ethical violations, suicide, and *incidents of domestic violence among police officers.*

The police subculture—often referred to as *the blue wall of silence, the blue curtain,* or the *thin blue line*--is believed to be the result of the strain that officers experience in their everyday police work attempting to reconcile their "crime fighter" mentality with the "public servant" and "social agent" demands placed upon them by society. A deep sense of cynicism can eventually develop in officers as a result of these challenges; as well as the complexity and uncertainty of their work environment. Although far from a legal excuse, this cynicism may shape police attitudes, values, and behaviors on the job.

Does police-perpetrated domestic violence truly occur in this country? According to scholars Terrill and Paoline (2003), *police-perpetrated domestic violence is estimated to occur in about 40% of all police families. Incredibly, this represents a rate that is approximately four times higher than that of non-police families!*

Admittedly, battering incidents in police families may differ somewhat from those of non-police families. How? Officers may be more knowledgeable and deft in the use of restraint holds and other physical techniques that leave no bruises or lacerations behind. *Coercion* in police families may also tend to be *less physical* and more psychological, emotional, and financial than in non-police families. Regardless, officer authority and control issues are clearly implicated in these offenses. Stressors related to the culture of law enforcement *itself* may play a role in the potential violence and coercion experienced in these relationships. An offending officer could well believe that he is "above the law" and "untouchable" where domestic violence is concerned, given his job, connections, and intricate knowledge of the law and the system. Another factor we need to consider is the sense of shame, secrecy, and helplessness suffered by police families in which these offenses occur—these can be profound; leaving the victimized police spouse and children believing that they may have nowhere in which to turn for help. Could this be the very *reason* that police battering continues? If so, the Body of Christ must reach out to these hurting people.

I have worked and interacted professionally with many men and women in the police ranks over the years; and overwhelmingly, they have been individuals of integrity and conviction. As a professor, I have also helped to educate many students across a number of universities who intend to enter the field of law enforcement. We are well-served by such persons, however, few would contest the statement that sworn officers who batter their spouses cannot be allowed to abuse the legitimate power vested in them by society; the police organization must remove these offenders from duty and prosecute them for their criminal acts.

If there is indeed a blue wall of silence within the police organization that contributes to police-perpetrated domestic violence, it must crumble and give way today. Officers who engage in domestic violence cannot be allowed to hide behind their badges—they are a black eye upon what is an otherwise noble profession.

Chapter Six:
The Lord Teaches and Redeems

ALTHOUGH DEEPLY SATISFYING TO ME on many levels, it was my work as a police matron that I would eventually leave in order to attend law school. It gratifies me to report that, the second time I applied to Albany Law School of Union University in Albany, New York, I received an acceptance letter. Afterward, I was then able to enroll in the part-time program there in order to begin working on my law doctorate.

In 2004, after seeing an advertisement in my local newspaper and spending some time in prayer, the Lord lead me to apply for an adjunct teaching position in the very same Criminal Justice Department in which I myself had studied at Hudson Valley Community College in Troy. The Department Chair seemed impressed with what I had accomplished since graduating with my AAS in Criminal Justice in 2000. Consequently, she called me in for an interview. Although at that point, I had not as of yet taught any *credited* academic classes in college, I did have some previous experience teaching particular populations.

In our interview, I explained that, in the late 1980's, I had served as a Program Counselor for the *New York State Supplemental Food Program for Women, Infants, and Children* (WIC Program), where I conducted individual and group counseling sessions disseminating *American Academy of Pediatrics* guidelines to diverse, economically-disadvantaged clients. To that end, I developed and taught nutrition and hygiene classes to children five and under; taught infant care to pregnant/parenting teenagers and post-partum adults; and also served as the Program's Lactation Consultant.

I also emphasized that, in the early 1990's, as a floral designer, I was the sole proprietor and craft teacher for *The Joshua Tree of Crafts & Floral Design*. For those five years, I'd created original fresh, silk, and dried floral arrangements for both my customers and local area businesses while also providing private floral design lessons for clients. During that time, I'd also taught craft classes for children and senior citizens as well as non-credit leisure time courses on floral design right on the campus of Hudson Valley Community College itself.

Finally, I pointed out that, after having had my sons, I then became a day care teacher. For those five years, from 1995 through 2000, I'd operated the *Tremblay Family Daycare*, a registered home-based business which provided full-time, part-time, and summer care to children of my clients, infants through the second grade. Lastly, I stressed how I had supervised and taught my clients' children as well as my own during the day while earning a criminal justice degree at HVCC in the evening.

After reviewing my work in the field, evaluating my prior teaching experience, and learning about my future plans to earn a law doctorate, she extended me an offer of employment. Happily, I was hired as faculty just prior to having completed my first master's degree (MS) in Criminal Justice. I knew the Lord had his Hand on me.

As an adjunct instructor and academic advisor, I went on to develop and teach undergraduate courses both on-campus and online for the Criminal Justice Department. In addition to teaching and advising students, I served as

Faculty Mentor and Education Specialist for the Center for Effective Teaching and would develop and manage *First-Year Success*, an organization in the HVCC portal for new faculty and distance learning instructors at the college. In order to expand my legal knowledge, I then served as Parliamentarian of the Academic Senate; researching relevant laws and ensuring that meetings of the Senate were conducted in accordance with *Robert's Rules of Order* and proper parliamentary procedure.

Not only did the Lord allow me to teach criminal justice and law classes each term, I was also able to assist students with their academic degree planning. Soon afterward, I was asked to develop and teach *College Forum*, a freshman seminar course intended to augment the basic research, writing, and academic skills of first-year, first-generation college students--many of whom were economically and educationally disadvantaged, as I myself once was.

In 2007, based upon my performance, I was invited to join the full-time faculty after teaching there for three years as an adjunct faculty member. I would next go on to teach five to six courses every fall and spring as well as a full-time load during the two summer terms. I then formed the *Criminal Justice Association*, a club for students interested in pursuing careers in the field of criminal justice. I also developed and delivered undergraduate courses across the Criminal Justice curriculum for the department, both on-campus and online, as well as supervised part-time faculty within their respective positions. The Lord continued to raise me up.

Based upon those experiences at HVCC, I was also hired to teach at several other colleges, both on-campus and online via distance learning. Over the past ten years, I have had the pleasure of teaching both undergraduate and graduate courses such as *Introduction to Forensic Psychology*;

Prof. Deborah A. Tremblay

Drugs and Society; Criminology; Introduction to Juvenile Delinquency; Substantive Criminal Law; Procedural Criminal Law; Introduction to Criminal Justice; Introduction to Sociology; Understanding Crime and Criminal Justice; Exploring Society; Family Violence and Abuse; Introduction to Psychology; Social Science Research Methods; Mental Health and the Law; Women, Health, and the Body; Police Stress and Mental Health; Social Implications of Medical Issues; Research in Counseling; Corrections; Psychology for Law Enforcement; as well as a number of others.

Another high point came for me when I was hired as faculty to teach several courses at *The Sage Colleges*, where I had once formerly worked for grocery money as a temporary cashier in *The Sage Colleges Bookstore*, and later as weekend closer; where I would go on to graduate with honors as a part-time student. The Lord had truly brought me full-circle.

I have since taught at several quality online institutions, and had the opportunity to supervise a course assistant for my *Introduction to Psychology* course from a distance. Together we collaborate and work toward the academic success and betterment of our students, who, much like we ourselves once did, juggle work, school, and family responsibilities in order to earn a college degree.

Over time, I have received many letters and emails from students, who, like me, have overcome much and are passionate about justice. They have worked hard to accomplish all that they have. Please allow me to share some of these online communications with you. I do this as a gesture to indicate how the Lord has been able to use *even* me.

'Dear Professor,

I am a good student because you helped me become a good student. You engaged me, and understood me. Perhaps my views were too real for some of my peers, but the things that I have seen through the eyes of an addict/prostitute and so much more are not seen with average eyes. I have entered crack houses. I lived in the streets and although I will only admit this to you, I did live in my car for one week until I got paid from work in order to move into my apartment. It's funny how I never told anyone this, not even my best friend. NEVER my family. Anyway, that was a different time in my life. God was looking out.

You know something professor, although I never met you face to face, I think that you are good at what you do. I mean, from my end, it seems that you meet your students where they are. You are not arrogant as some professors can be. Perhaps you had humble beginnings; I don't mean economically, or perhaps so, but I think you worked hard to get what you have and it's well deserved. Keep yourself the down-to-earth person that I know you are. Well this is my very little insight into you, without having actually met you or spent time with you. I would be interested in knowing if I am right, wrong, or close. I have one more term before graduation—yippee and yahoo! Take care.'

'Professor Tremblay,

I dedicate this essay to Prof. Tremblay, who probably has no idea how much she has influenced my life during this past semester. The last year has been filled with stresses I have never dreamed would surface. My own health issues, along with the psychological problems involving my oldest daughter, have caused our close-knit family to struggle to keep our seams together. My job loss was something I never thought would occur, forcing both my wife and me to take extra courses. Nobody wants to lose the house they worked so hard to purchase. I began this class with trepidation about my lack of knowledge of psychology; apprehensive about what I could accomplish. After taking this class, my speaking, writing, and understanding have improved. I feel less timid about expressing and defending my opinions about issues, as I did with this essay. Multiple kudos to Professor Tremblay and her assistant. I thank you and tip my hat to you as I shall never forget this class, nor you!'

'Dear Professor,

This class has been both interesting and difficult for me. I am an incest survivor and have reached a point in my life where I feel like a "healthy" individual. I have worked hard in my life to break the cycle of abuse that has been in my family for years. It has not been an easy or short road but I have come to the other end in better shape than when I started. This course had moments of stirring up feelings that I thought were long gone <u>but</u> I am glad I did this. I have learned a lot and found I am stronger than I thought. Thank you for your support that was given throughout the class.'

'Professor,

I am getting ready to go into the police academy for a local police department. This course has been helpful, interesting, and realistic. This course has opened my eyes up to warning signs, risk factors, and preventative measures for dealing with stress on the job. The research on stress and mental health issues gave me insight into the police profession that will make me more aware of the police subculture (both positive and negative). Most importantly, I gave great thought about the article on reactive vs. proactive policing. I had never really thought about police officers like that before, but it is completely true. I want to be as proactive as possible because otherwise, I don't think you are completely protecting your community. I have learned that it is important to keep open communication with friends and family, not to become cynical, use healthy and positive ways to relieve stress, and seek assistance if ever faced with a mental health issue.'

'Professor Tremblay,

I decided to study law after one of your lectures this semester. I want to pursue a career in juvenile justice, which is what I realized I wanted to do after taking your class. It's been a hard couple of years with everything that has been going on, but I finally see my life coming back on track. (Thank God). I would like to try to take at least one of your classes next semester, so I will be looking forward to that. I also want to say thank you for all your help and encouragement. I enjoyed your classes and I haven't yet found a teacher that makes their students enjoy class as much as you do. Thank you!'

I also currently teach synchronous distance learning classes over my home computer for another institution; where my students and I meet online at pre-arranged times, in weekly audio lectures utilizing a microphone, camera, and whiteboard with which to interact. I have learned that, while the *face* of education may have changed somewhat, the *heart* of it has remained very much the same.

It has been very gratifying to be able to help educate and empower many men and women over the years as they have pursued their own deeply-held dreams and goals. Suffice it to say--little do my students know that I have learned far more from them than they ever have from me. Thank you, ladies and gentlemen. I give you all a heartfelt A+. May Jesus bless each and every one of you.

Chapter Seven:
Hard Lessons on Domestic Violence

I AM SAD TO SAY that one of my very first memories as a toddler is an image of my father shoving my mother as I sat observing from my high chair in our kitchen. Years later, in what could have been one of my very last memories, a bed pillow was coming down over my face as my first husband attempted to strangle and suffocate me on our bed in our bedroom. I never connected these two events until very recently—although on an *extremely* wide continuum, how are they related?

As I teach my students today, domestic violence, or what is often referred to as *battering*, is not a private family matter but a crime. The batterer seeks to establish dominance, power, and control over another through fear, intimidation, and the threat of or actual use of physical or sexual abuse. Abuse can also include behaviors that are less physical but more psychological or even economic in nature. In either case, the batterer or abuser believes that he or she is entitled to control their partner and that the abused is the "property" of the abuser. The abuser also believes that the violence used or abuse applied is a legitimate means of wielding that control.

Domestic violence is believed to be the most common yet least reported crime in the United States of America. Such abuse is vastly underreported in our country. **Easily, over six million American women are beaten each year by**

their male partners and over four thousand women are killed as a result of domestic violence every year. *I am convinced that I myself would have been one of those very women back in 1985 had the Lord not freed me from my first husband's grip.*

We also know that many men who abuse their spouses also often abuse their own children, stepchildren, or their partner's children. Sadly, children from abusive homes are much more likely to perpetuate the cycle of violence as adults in their own homes. What exactly is the *cycle of violence*?

According to domestic violence expert and my former NSU professor Dr. Lenore Walker, (with whom I worked on the asylum case from Costa Rica), and who first proposed that domestic violence was cyclical (*The Battered Woman*, 1979), the cycle of violence is conceptualized in three distinct phases: phase one is the *tension-building stage*; phase two is the *acute battering incident stage*; and phase three is the *kindness and contrite loving behavior stage*, or what has been termed the "*honeymoon stage.*" During the tension-building stage, minor battering incidents occur, but these are most often minimized by the victim, who instinctively understands that the batterer is capable of much more violence than he has utilized to that point. Phase one may last for several months or several years.

Phase two involves an uncontrollable discharge of violence and represents the culmination of phase one tensions. The batterer is enraged and the victim becomes the recipient of a severe physical assault. This phase generally lasts from two to twenty-four hours, although longer periods have indeed been reported.

What immediately follows in phase three are the batterer's attempts to reconcile with the victim; this period is characterized by an unusual period of calm during which the batterer displays superficial charm and remorse. At the same time, the batterer is generous, dependable, helpful, and genuinely interested in his partner. This *honeymoon* period does not last long, however, and the relationship is soon in the midst of the *tension-building phase* once again. The cycle then repeats itself, with each subsequent cycling period becoming more rapid as well as more intense.

While Dr. Walker's cycle of violence explains the dynamics at work in the batterer-victim relationship, *why* does the victim continue to remain within the cycle? Dr. Walker explains that the contrite behavior of the batterer in the honeymoon phase acts as a *behavioral reinforcement* to the victim's participation in the cycle, and that once established, a sense of *learned helplessness* accounts for the victim's perceived inability to escape this cycle. It would seem that both behavioral reinforcement and learned helplessness would take a significant period of time in which to develop. In that case, what can explain why a woman who is *newly* battered by her husband or significant other remains in the relationship *prior* to the cycle having been established?

I have often wondered if the cycle of violence in battering relationships were conceptualized with phase one as the *honeymoon phase*; phase two as the *tension-building phase*; and phase three as the *acute battering phase*, might this shift better explain why the battery victim endures both the *tension-building* and *acute battering phases*? I respectfully asked Dr. Walker her opinion of this cycle shift when I was her student at NSU. (Happily, not only did she graciously consider my question, but took no offense, and actually allowed me to pass her class!)

Think about the dynamics of a marriage relationship in its early stages. Often referred to itself as the "honeymoon period," this stage of a relationship is characterized by a high degree of physical, sexual, and emotional attraction between the couple. Both persons tend to "idealize" the other; maximizing each person's positive attributes while minimizing each other's negative ones. During this stage of the relationship, the potential batterer convinces the future victim that he alone is able to meet her needs. This promotes her gradual but complete reliance upon him, and she is susceptible to his suggestions that she can only safely place her trust in him. He may manipulate her into avoiding certain associates and companions, working fewer hours, visiting family less, and will generally seek to promote his agenda of fulfilling the majority of her emotional and psychological needs. Having spent considerable time and effort portraying the "man of her dreams," his eventual displays of jealousy, possessiveness, and ever-increasing control are perceived by the victim as evidence of "love" and "desire."

The first time her partner strikes her, she experiences genuine bewilderment. How can this "perfect" man have reacted in such a manner? Clearly, she believes she *must* be the one at fault; she has committed an offense that has stirred his "legitimate" wrath. She becomes persuaded of this "truth," while the batterer seizes the opportunity to exert ever-increasing control over aspects of both her personal and professional lives. He may then begin a subtle campaign to sabotage her professional success and autonomy, with the goal of undermining her independence and jeopardizing her employment. Her world necessarily becomes smaller and smaller until eventually nothing remains in it except himself. The cycle of violence may then go forward, with the victim forever anticipating the return of the "man of her dreams," a complete fiction created by the batterer.

As a student and professor, I have studied and taught several variations of Dr. Walker's work, yet have never come across any theory that improves upon hers nor better explains the crime of domestic violence.

Again, domestic violence is not a private family matter, but a crime. Accordingly, many states have enacted mandatory arrest laws in the case of domestic violence. Consider the mandatory arrest policy of the state of New York (2002), N.Y. CPLR. Art. 140.10(4), first enacted in 1994. This statute provides that when probable cause exists to find that a family offense felony has been committed by an individual against another member of the same family or household, a law enforcement officer "... shall arrest a person, and shall not attempt to reconcile the parties or mediate." In the case where an order of protection is in effect which directs the defendant to stay away from the victim and the defendant acts in violation of that "stay away" provision, an arrest is also to be made. When a family offense misdemeanor has been committed, an arrest is to be made unless the victim requests otherwise. The statute reads, "The officer shall neither inquire as to whether the victim seeks an arrest of such person nor threaten the arrest of any person for the purpose of discouraging requests for police intervention."

When an officer has probable cause to believe that more than one family member or household member has committed such a misdemeanor, the officer is not required to arrest *each* person. He or she is required to, "attempt to identify and arrest the primary physical aggressor" by considering "the comparative extent of any injuries;" whether either party "is threatening or has threatened future harm" against the other or another family or household member; whether either party "has a prior history of domestic violence;" and whether either party acted "defensively to protect himself or herself from injury." (Probable cause is a reasonably-based belief; based upon facts and circumstances within the officer's knowledge, that two things have occurred—first, that a specific crime has been committed, and secondly, that a particular person has committed that crime. Probable cause is necessary for all lawful arrests.) The statute further provides that the officer, "evaluate each complaint separately to determine who...the primary physical aggressor [is]" and that the officer "shall not base the decision to arrest or not to arrest on the willingness of [one] person to testify" against the other. The officer is also required to prepare and file a written report of the domestic violence incident on a specialized form following the investigation and include statements from both the victim and witnesses, whether an arrest is made or not. The report is to be "retained by the law enforcement agency for a period of not less than four years."

As I teach my students, the legislative intent behind mandatory arrest policies is to both remove the decision to press criminal charges against a batterer from the battered victim, as well as to require that an arrest be made in lieu of informal mediation or other police intervention when a domestic violence episode occurs and is reported within a particular jurisdiction.

Historically, domestic violence had often been viewed as a "family" or "personal" issue by law enforcement, not warranting the formal intervention of law enforcement agencies. The definitive societal trend in recent history to recognize domestic violence as *criminal behavior* has been observed both at the local and national levels in this country. Through the efforts of women's rights groups, scholars, criminologists, sociologists, psychologists, lobbyists, public officials, educators, social service agencies, and domestic violence advocacy groups, as well as others, the campaign to view domestic violence less as a family or social problem that occurs behind "closed doors" has effectively "changed the face" of domestic violence in the eyes of mainstream society.

Although the law has often been slow to evolve in areas of social concern--absent a groundswell of reaction and public outcry that fuel such change--domestic violence has, as a matter of public policy in recent years, finally been recognized for the criminal and legal problem that it is. Unfortunately, as we also know, in the past, victims of domestic violence had often been far too frightened and intimidated by the presence of their batterer to press formal charges even after police were summoned--a sense of *learned helplessness* would set in as these domestic violence victims would perceive that no legal remedy or recourse existed for them; and that their batterer was "untouchable."

The New York State Legislature also recently responded to the crime of manual strangulation, with *The Strangulation Prevention Act of 2010*, enacted on November 11, 2010. The new law established three new criminal offenses: first, second, and third degree strangulation. The text of the new statute follows:

Section 120.73 Strangulation in the first degree:

A person is guilty of strangulation in the first degree when, with intent to cause physical injury or to place such other person in reasonable fear of physical injury, serious physical injury or death, he or she cause physical injury to such other person or causes such other person to lose consciousness for any period of time by means of applying pressure on the throat or neck of such other person by means of blocking the nose or mouth of such other person or by a combination of such means. Strangulation in the first degree is a Class C Felony.

Section 120.72 Strangulation in the second degree:

A person is guilty of strangulation in the second degree when he or she intentionally places or attempts to place another person in reasonable fear of physical injury, serious physical injury or death by impairing or impeding for any period of time the normal breathing or blood circulation of such other person by means of intentionally applying pressure on the throat or neck of such other person or by means of intentionally blocking the nose or mouth of such other person, or by any combination of such means. Strangulation in the second degree is a Class E Felony.

Section 120.71 Strangulation in the third degree:

1. A person is guilty of strangulation in the third degree when, with intent to impair, impede, or otherwise interfere with the normal breathing or blood circulation of another person, he or she applies pressure on the throat or neck of such other person or blocks the nose or mouth of such other person, or both, in a manner that impairs or impedes, for any period of time, the normal breathing or blood circulation of such other person. 2. Conduct performed for a valid medical or dental purpose shall not constitute a violation of subdivision one of this section. Strangulation in the third degree is a Class A Misdemeanor.

Unfortunately, prior to the new law, absent any obvious visible physical evidence of manual strangulation, prosecutors had little recourse but to reduce the criminal charges against the domestic violence perpetrator to that of non-criminal harassment, (considered a *violation* rather than a crime), particularly in the case where no visible physical injury appeared to exist at the time of the offense. Ironically, however, manual strangulation leaves no physical injuries immediately afterward--the tell-tale bruising from such an attack takes hours or *even as long as days* to appear upon the neck of the victim. Since the crime of strangulation has been added to the *NYS Penal Law*, it is estimated that more than two thousand suspects have been arrested as a result, since strangulation that results in injury or unconsciousness to the victim is now considered a violent felony under the law. The law also seeks to ensure that a convicted offender will either remain behind bars or under supervision for life—*anyone convicted of either felony or misdemeanor counts must submit a DNA sample to authorities.* **Many advocates support the new statute--pointing out that strangulation, a very common form of aggravated assault in domestic violence--can frequently lead to brain damage.** It is commonly understood that, from a medical standpoint, when a victim is strangled, he or she typically experiences severe pain; followed then by unconsciousness; afterward resulting in a degree of brain death.

According to Amy Barasch, executive director of the New York State Office for the Prevention of Domestic Violence, (http://www.opdv.state.ny.us), as many as forty four percent of all women killed within my home state of New York in 2009 (the most recent year that statistics were published online by this organization) have died as the direct result of battering in intimate violence incidents. Furthermore, women in abusive relationships who are subsequently strangled by their abuser are, statistically speaking, ten times more likely to be killed by them at some future point.

Exactly how many victims were killed via intimate partner abuse by manual strangulation in New York during 1985? Although I may not be able to say so definitively; I can state the following with certainty: **As I recalled the purple**

Prof. Deborah A. Tremblay

handprints that had once encircled my neck at the hands of my attacker over 26 years ago, I have little doubt that--except for God's direct intervention—I would have been one of them.

Chapter Eight:
Seizures: Trapped in Twilight

IN SOME REGARDS, *I FEEL like I don't know where I have been for the past three years.* It is almost as though part of me has been lost; although I still have a wealth of memories to treasure—other vital recollections seem to be missing—almost as if they've never been formed to begin with. I have learned from a medical standpoint that not only can no memories be formed during a seizure; *but the seizures themselves can often result in short-term memory loss.*

Nocturnal seizure disorder, just as the term implies, occurs during sleep. According to the *Winthrop-University Hospital* Website, 'nocturnal or sleep-related seizures can cause abnormal movement or behavior during sleep. They are a form of epilepsy caused by abnormal electrical activity within the brain. They frequently occur in people with epileptic seizures during the day, but may also occur only at night. Symptoms range from awakening many times a night for no apparent reason to violent movements of the arms and legs accompanied by tongue biting and bedwetting.'

According to the *Mayo Clinic's* Website at (http://www.mayoclinic.com/health/grand-mal-seizure/DS00222), grand mal seizure, or what is often referred to as a, "tonic-clonic seizure:"

'...features a loss of consciousness and violent muscle contractions. It's the type of seizure most people picture when they think about seizures in general. Grand mal seizure is caused by abnormal electrical activity throughout the brain. In some cases, this type of seizure is triggered by other health problems, such as extremely low blood sugar or a stroke. However, most of the time grand mal seizure is caused by epilepsy. Many people who have a grand mal seizure will never have another one. However, some people need daily anti-seizure medications to control grand mal seizure.'

Comparatively speaking, the *Mayo Clinic's* Website at (http://www.mayoclinic.com/health/petit-mal-seizure/DS00216) also describes a petit mal, or an absence seizure (what I have frequently referred to as a, "blip") as involving:

'...a brief, sudden lapse of consciousness. Absence seizures are more common in children than adults. Someone having an absence seizure may look like he or she is staring into space for a few seconds. Compared with other types of epileptic seizures, absence seizures appear mild. But they can be dangerous. Children with a history of absence seizure must be supervised carefully while swimming or bathing because of the danger of drowning. Teens and adults may be restricted from driving and other potentially hazardous activities.'

Owing to these seizure events, I feel as though part of me has been taken away, and there are no words that can adequately begin to address this sense of loss. While my long-term memories are very clear, aspects of my short-term memory have been snatched away by the seizures. In some respects, I have been robbed of these very rich memories. ***Several times, I have gone to retrieve a precious memory concerning my children and, much like one coming upon an empty vault; I have found***

that the most valuable possessions I own have been stolen from me. At other times, have been much more readily able to recall events and occasions that have transpired forty years ago than to be able to remember what has occurred merely four years ago.

Over these past few years, it is as though I have been trapped in a complex spiritual, emotional, and cognitive labyrinth through which I have been unable to find my way--returning again and again to the very point at which I first started. Fortunately, as I have wound my way throughout a veritable corn maze of confusion, at every confounding pathway and each twisted turn; even in the face of my innermost quandary, the Lord has assured me that He can and will, 'restore what the locusts have eaten.'

I had always believed that I could rely upon my intellect, my education, and my reason to see me through the challenges I have been faced with over these past several years. I believed that I could rely upon my own strength and the attributes that the Lord has given me when these difficulties arose in my life. What I have learned is that, it is the Lord and His strength that I need to rely upon—were it not for Him, I honestly believe that I would not be able to go on.

As loving, caring, and supportive as my family has been during this time, they cannot fully know what I have experienced nor can I expect them to. (Just as aspects of what they have experienced are lost on me as they have watched me go through these processes.) Sadly, however, I have noticed that those around me do tend to treat me somewhat differently since I began suffering seizures. Of course, it is most certainly out of love and concern that they do so, yet to have one's actions, words, decisions, and behaviors questioned where they never were before is both heartrending and humbling. From a human standpoint, this has undermined my confidence and esteem. I also deeply regret the pain, fear, and concern that I have caused my husband and sons. It has been hard on all of us yet the only One Who truly understands what we have all been through is the Lord Himself.

Additionally, my sense of time has been taken hostage. Time seems to have slowed down considerably. I experience the passage of time much differently than I used to; often I believe that an event has transpired a very long time ago, while it has only occurred very recently. At a recent visit to a counselor, I was stunned to learn from my husband that I had experienced a grand mal seizure only weeks earlier—I was convinced it had been several months since I had seized. Needless to say, this has affected my self-perception: can I truly trust what I believe I perceive?

Of that very first seizure event, my husband Matt writes:

'It came like a thief in the night in March 2009 around 2:00am. Deb had her first grand mal seizure. I didn't know what it was called at the time or what exactly was happening. Those first five minutes were terrifying; I thought I was losing my best friend and the center of my life for the past twenty-five years. Later that day in the ER, after many tests, the doctor confirmed that it was a seizure but, thank the Lord, not caused by any major physical problem like a tumor or an aneurism.

'That night over two years ago has affected our family and me in many ways. I worry about Deb. I worry for her health; both short term and long term. I worry about the injury that each seizure or blip may be causing her brain. I worry about the boys; especially Jake. He takes each event hard—it hurts him to see his mom going through them. I worry that Deb may get hurt in some other way; falling down, or pneumonia from aspiration.

'I worry how this has consumed Deb—she has lived with this every minute of each day. She has beaten herself up for a quarter of century due to her brief relationship with an abuser. I feel sadness and pain over Deb's lost memories of the past two years and her loss of independence in being unable to jump in her car and drive where she wants or needs to go. I am recalling the times she has had to think twice about attending a social event; going out of the house; or even having to change her plans. It also hurts me to see her frequently staring out of the window, knowing that she longs to be out there, a part of it.

'Obviously, I am not happy about these seizure events, nor do I want them to continue. If I can take any positive from this experience, however, it is that the Lord has opened my eyes to other things He is doing in our lives; He has brought us closer in our relationship. He provided the tools and opportunities for her to work from home and still do what she loves; teaching students and touching their lives in so many ways. She works for herself, and has been able to provide a structured and supportive environment to home school our three youngest sons. (They have thrived!) I myself feel closer to the Lord; I talk to Him many times during the day. What is my position on all of this? I pray for Deb's healing and deliverance; I have faith in the Lord that He will heal and deliver; in His own time and way.'

My son Josh, now aged 28, shares:

'I didn't know much about brain seizures or the impact that a domestic violence attack could have on an individual's life until my mother began experiencing them as a result of a brutal strangulation that occurred in 1985; perpetrated by her first husband. I've known my mother long enough to be familiar with how she usually behaves and what she normally says. When she started having seizures about three years ago, my family and I were in shock because we didn't know what was happening or what could be causing the seizures.

'Dad and I went to the hospital with her and the doctors ran tests; concluding that she should be on seizure medication. The medication prescribed caused her to feel like she was wading through water or as if in a dream or fog whenever she tried to move or to speak. My mother is a professor at several colleges and found she couldn't function as before while on this medication.

'Since then, the grand mal seizures have greatly decreased--it has been about a month since her last grand mal seizure, but another type (petite mal) seems to have taken its place. This is the type my mother has referred to as, "blips." These are actually complex partial seizures in which she says and does things she has no memory of and appears to, "check out," for as long as several minutes at a time. Some of it has to do with reliving the day in 1985 when she was brutally strangled by her first husband. During these events she is not herself. There's a darker side to this—a spiritual evil seems to be exerted over her whenever she experiences a blip.

'The good news is that the seizures have lessened; however, when she has experienced petit mal seizures in the past two to three months, it's as though she has "checked out" and something that is definitely not her has "checked in"—as if using her voice and body. I am a Christian, and while talking to my mother, I could discern that the Holy Spirit wasn't speaking to me—whatever it was, is evil. I can see that this is a spiritual problem, not merely a biological, psychological, or medical one. Spiritual weapons are necessary to fight it. With faith and trust in God we defeat Satan; freeing ourselves from the consequences of our past actions (as my mother described in this book.) Please pray for my mother, my family, and me as we go through this struggle. We know God always has the victory--my mother will be free.'

My son Caleb, now aged 21, observes:

'Over the past few years, I have observed my mother go through the difficult and often painful process of coming to terms with unfortunate limitations imposed upon her life by an unforeseen and definitely unwanted obstacle— epilepsy. As she has undergone this journey, I have tried to walk with her and to do what I can to help her as she has struggled to understand what the seizures have meant for her family and her.

'Initially, my reaction to the seizures was that of terror. To witness one in the throes of a seizure can be frightening, especially if you are unfamiliar with what is happening. The person having the seizure might make a yelling noise as her body contorts, followed by a period of heavy breathing while the body goes rigid and the eyes remain open. There is nothing an observer can do to help but try to prevent that person from hurting herself until the episode is concluded. When my mother first began having seizures at night, I was frightened and confused; but now as time has gone on and I understand the phenomena of epilepsy a little better, my fears have largely dissipated, though I maintain a reasonable concern for my mother.

'On one level, I am concerned about my mother's physical health. While she is having a seizure, there is a chance that she might bite her tongue or aspirate saliva, causing an infection. Additionally, after the seizure has concluded, my mother's senses and strength remain impaired for a short period of time, increasing the chances that she might stumble over an object and fall.

'In addition to these concerns, the risk of physical danger during "blips' (which occur more frequently than full-fledged tonic clonic seizures) must also be acknowledged. While my mother is undergoing what she calls a, "blip," she loses control of her body to some degree—she speaks jumbled phrases, her awareness of her environment is impaired, and she performs involuntary repetitive actions. If a, "blip" were to occur while she was driving, for example, it is not hard to imagine that she could get into a car accident. (For this reason, she does not drive.) Additionally, like other types of seizures, no memory of the, "blip" can be formed. The only way for my mother to know if she has had one is for another family member to tell her some time after it has occurred. As you can imagine, no one looks forward to informing her of this bad news, and I know that my mother is distraught when we have to tell her that this type of seizure has occurred. Unfortunately, this is a difficult circumstance that we are all trying to deal with the best we can.

'Perhaps more disconcerting, however, than the risks to physical health, is the negative impact of the stress of undergoing seizures and the resulting memory loss. Since my mother has been reflecting upon her past in an effort to understand the roots of these seizures, it has been difficult to see her suffer from emotional wounds stemming back to the abuses she suffered in her youth and early adulthood. The impact upon her memory is also difficult to witness, because although she still possesses the same high level of intelligence that she always has, her sense of chronology and her ability to call to mind concrete events of the recent past have both been affected.

'For me as a young man, to witness my mother, who has always been a foundation of support in my life as well as a very independent spirit, be made physically weak in instances and be rendered totally dependent upon others as she has a seizure, has been a shock and something that I have had to adjust to. I have gotten to the point where her actual seizures no longer disturb me, but I am still as concerned as ever as she suffers from the burden of events that her illness has had upon her life.'

My son Jeremiah, now aged 18, explains:

'I was six days away from turning fifteen when my mother had her first seizure. I was awakened during those early morning hours when the seizure occurred. I heard a loud, long shout and, at first, it sounded to me as if someone was having a nightmare. As I left my bedroom, I glanced over into the living room, where my mother was sleeping on the couch. I looked on in horror and disbelief as she shook and convulsed; her body and limbs rigid. It became clear to me that she had shouted. I tore my eyes away and ran to get my father. I told him that my mother was having what I thought was most likely a seizure, and we both ran to her side. By then, my brothers Daniel and Jacob were both awake as well.

'My father held my mother steady to prevent her from falling from the couch and asked for tissues to wipe the saliva away from her mouth. For some reason, I grabbed the family camcorder at the same time, knowing my mother would want me to, although I was still too panicked to turn it on. At that point, several thoughts shot through my mind: What was happening to my mother? Why was it this happening? Would she suffer any physical or mental injury from this event? I had heard of seizures, but had never witnessed one before, nor was I aware of their aftereffects.

'After a few minutes, the convulsions stopped, and my mother proceeded to wake up, confused. She wandered throughout the house, performing actions that were practically second nature to her because she had probably performed them thousands of times in her life; she then began folding laundry and emptying the washing machine. It was at this point that I finally gathered the courage up to start recording what was happening.

'My father brought her back to the couch, and began asking her several questions. Slowly, her full awareness of herself and others returned, and we explained the situation to her, with the camera rolling the whole time. After talking for awhile, they determined she should visit the hospital in the morning. At that point, I stopped recording, deciding that I had captured what I needed to and had a good idea of what had happened. (Neither I, nor anyone else, have watched that footage since I recorded it. In fact, I don't feel a need to watch it; it is unfortunately still as fresh in my mind as it was when I witnessed it through the lens of the camera.)

'Slowly, we all eventually returned to bed that night, but none of us could sleep. None could know just how significant this event would be in our lives, especially my mother's. However, there is no doubt in my now seventeen-year-old mind that this situation is temporary; I find peace in knowing that this terrible occurrence is metamorphosing into a meaningful testimony that, no doubt, will reach many. The answers will come in time.'

Daniel, now aged 16, writes:

'When my mom had her first seizure, I remember us all violently trembling in fear. I can still remember the horror of seeing her convulsing and foaming at the mouth on the living room couch. It was 3:30 in the morning. My younger brother, Jacob, was also awakened by the commotion. My older brother, Jeremiah, had heard her having the seizure and ran to get my father. My dad woke me and had me come into the living room to help him. Mom was convulsing in such a way that she had closed her lips together and was blowing hard; we all stayed with her until she was responsive. She didn't want to call 911; I wondered if we should; especially since we had no idea what was going on at first. What was happening to our mother?

'Two years have passed since then, and she has improved significantly. She has seizures much less often and they do not last as long. They are much less violent. It made me realize how precious life is, and how we take being healthy for granted. In some ways, this experience has shown me how to behave more adult-like. I find I behave much more maturely with my family and friends, offering support when they go through hard times. I also make it clear to everyone that seizures are nothing to joke about. Has this experience been an easy one? No. Did I enjoy going through it? No. But, has it changed me? Yes, and for the better. All things happen for a reason, and God can help you no matter what.'

Jacob, now aged 13, recalls:

'How has this situation affected me? Every day I worry about my mom. Whenever a friend comes over, I fear she may have a blip. I also feel badly for her when she is upset about a blip or a seizure. Every night I pray that she will be healed and that this will stop.'

Prof. Deborah A. Tremblay

To my husband Matthew and sons Joshua, Caleb, Jeremiah, Daniel, and Jacob: thank you for your love, faithfulness, support, and strength every day, but especially throughout this difficult time. Not only have you shown me the true meaning of the word *family*, but you six men have individually taught me what *true manhood* and Christ-like character is all about. I love, respect, and admire each of you.

Chapter Nine:
Lessons From Childhood

HAVE YOU EVER PONDERED HOW small and vulnerable we are on our own? These days, I often feel just like a young child who has gotten lost or been abandoned in a department store--frightened and very much alone. It was well over forty years ago when I first got lost in a department store while out shopping with my grandmother, aunt, and cousin in Menands, a town located just outside of my current city of Watervliet, New York. Back before the atriums and malls here in the 1970's, the store was known as *Two Guys*. In the store's basement, trembling and fighting rising panic, I pressed the elevator's button for the first floor, my fears rising as rapidly as the store's escalator as I desperately searched for a familiar face. Amidst a crowd of strangers, I wandered aisles of silent, mocking mannequins; my six year-old heart beating frantically against my chest the entire time.

In the present, whenever I have been driven by that same lot, I have stolen a glance over, reminded of that day I became separated from my Nana; the sense of blameworthiness I experienced and how small, vulnerable, and frightened I had suddenly become. After all these years, memories of that episode are fresh within my 48-year-old heart and mind; I still recall how lost, alone, and utterly terrified I was on my own after having foolishly lost hold of my grandmother.

At times, I experience that self-same terror as I cry out to My Heavenly Father in the midst of my adult loneliness, confusion, pain, and fear after having broken away from and failed to follow after Him. Although He has promised to never leave me nor forsake me, isn't it me who has become emotionally and psychologically separated, distant, and far-removed from Him; much like a frightened child lost and alone in a department store--ever trying to discover her way back?

Prior to the time that I determined that I should no longer operate my vehicle until I receive a "clean bill of health;" I was out driving with my now 18-year-old son, Jeremiah, who had accompanied me on an errand. Close to home here in Watervliet, lies a piece of property which, for a time, also housed a vacant, empty lot; now currently rented out to several small government office buildings. Each time I had come off the highway ramp and driven past this area, I had peered over and tried to recall where a particular department store had been situated back in the 1970's. My grandparents--Nana and Pop—had taken my cousin Cheri and I shopping there many times prior to their weekly grocery shopping jaunts just across the street at the *Price Chopper* supermarket.

As Jeremiah and I drove by, I signaled with my directional then pulled into the department store's abandoned lot. To my knowledge, that was the first time I had been on that property since I had last been in Nana's and Pop's *Buick*. To me, it had always represented much more just than a fond memory to which I might return; but a gateway of security through which I could time-travel or a bridge of stability over which I could pass to reach an ultimate sense of safety.

"I would just like to see if I can determine where this store was actually located," I told my son. He nodded with understanding beyond his years. I had mentioned the store on a previous trip, and decided we could now afford to borrow some time (if not steal a few moments) from our present lives in order to revisit the past. I swung my car around into the lot, only guessing at where I believed the store to have been. After four decades, I couldn't be certain.

"I know it was somewhere over here," I heard myself utter. "But where? Lord, please show me." My eyes were drawn upward. There, on the outside of the building directly across from where we had parked, was a very subtle yet distinctive *Two Guys* watermark outline from store signage that had long-since been removed. It was noteworthy to me that, like my faded but clear memories, it, too, had weathered many a storm. Thinking about my current circumstances, I then had to wonder: *Could I not weather this one?*

A little later that same week, I had driven to my Nana's and Pop's old home; the one in which they had lived during the 1970's, and the home I had essentially grown up in. During the time I had lived with both of my parents as a very young child; or my mother as a pre-teen following their divorce; or my father as a teenager after several custody issues, Nana's old home had remained the one true constant. Perhaps I was searching for the familiar, the only place I had ever truly thought of as my, 'home.' There in my car, I reminisced about the many holidays and occasions my brother, sisters, cousins, relatives, and I had celebrated there; the sound of my Uncle Jeff's piano-playing, the unwrapping of gifts, and the din of laughter echoing throughout my memories.

As I did so, I marveled at how my grandmother could do culinary magic in that very kitchen; taking the simplest of ingredients and creating dishes that were like no one else's. Her homemade spaghetti sauce was a family favorite. It would simmer all day long on Sunday, filling that house with an aroma that made our mouths water. As for her meatballs—I was convinced they were straight from Heaven's menu.

"Nana, how do you make them taste so good?" I had once asked her.

"The trick," she confided, "is in the mixing."

As a young girl, I'd set the meat, cheese, onions, eggs, garlic, oregano, olive oil, bread crumbs and other items beside her glass mixing bowl for her and she'd combine everything without measuring; adding a pinch of this or a handful of that. When it came time to mix, she would work her hands down into the bowl, until the spices and seasonings were all perfectly blended. As she rolled the meatballs and began cooking them in olive oil, she'd often observe, "Meatballs are a lot like life; each has its own ingredients that give it flavor. Both are messy too, but you should never be afraid to put yourself in the mix, wouldn't you say?" She'd then chuckle and wink at me. In spite of myself, I nodded. That memory brought a smile to my face—even with the serious issues I now faced *today*, those words heartened me.

Eventually, I began to drive away, dabbing at tears.

Not too far away, just across the street from the local firehouse, was the old neighborhood playground. I again decided to pull my car off of the road there and park. My smile returned as my mind went back to the day, when, as a girl, I hung upside down from the monkey bars in that very park, daydreaming about a costume party to which I had been invited and fantasizing about modeling the princess costume my mother had prepared for me.

As I had hung there, I noticed two older boys marching through the park playing a game of, *Follow the Leader.* Awestruck, I had watched as the first boy climbed to the top of the sliding board, then rode easily down on his feet while the second boy then followed, "surfing" down as effortlessly as his Leader had.

True to my tomboy impulses, I had yearned to try their trick. I distinctly recalled bounding over to that slide and purposefully scaling its steps. At the top of the sliding board, my heart beat wildly. Locking my knees and extending my arms for flight, I boldly ventured down.

Fly I did—off the end of the sliding board, face-first into the rocky dirt. For a time I lay there, stunned and winded; my chest a painful, empty cavity. Once I could finally draw full breaths again, I rose and ran home crying, my body battered and my ego bruised. After a trip to the doctor, I bathed, had dinner, and settled down to bed.

When the morning of the costume party had arrived, I awoke and excitedly slipped into the princess gown and bejeweled golden crown my mother had designed for me. Eagerly, I sought the full-length mirror. Unfortunately, when I took in my reflection, my visions of regal splendor were shattered--beneath my right eye was the meanest looking shiner I could imagine. I was horrified! I resembled much more the *Beast*, rather than the *Beauty* I had envisioned.

When my mother saw my black eye back then, she, too, had been taken aback. I was too busy feeling sorry for myself to notice her fatigue from having worked late into the night preparing my costume. I could only think of myself and how my own hopes had been dashed. My mother studied me for a few moments. Then she smiled. "Don't worry," she assured me, "I know what to do."

At the kitchen table, she designed a pale-green silky dress whose sleeves were shaped just like leaves. Next, she fashioned a large, lightweight headpiece that tied under my chin and framed my face with satiny golden-yellow flower petals. She worked carefully and skillfully, all morning long. As I watched and waited on her, my wilting spirits decidedly began to lift.

When my new costume was ready, my mother helped me with the fitting. She stood back and after scrutinizing the effect, went to her room and promptly returned with her make-up bag. Cupping my chin in her hand, she gently outlined my blackened eye with a dark eyebrow pencil. When she had finished, my black eye had become my greatest asset.

I still recall our reflections in the mirror as we admired her handiwork.

"You're not a girl with a black eye," she insisted as she had adjusted my costume's headpiece.

"What am I?" I had tentatively sniffed.

She had placed her hand on my shoulder. "You're a perennial Black-Eyed Susan; by far, the most unique of all flowers."

A seed was planted deep within me at that moment; I sensed God's touch in my mother's gifted hand. At that time, rather than shame, I had felt...honor.

After awhile, my mind had come back to the present. As I pulled my car back onto the road and headed for home, I thought about the life I had lived since that time, and prayed that My Father's redemptive touch could once again take away the sense of shame I still bore for having been treated so disdainfully by my first husband, and the manner in which he had abused my son Joshua and me. All these years later, I knew that only He could heal both the physical seizures as well as that abiding sense of *shame* I long suffered—*it had been nothing less than a black-eye upon my emotional countenance.*

During this remarkable healing process, the Lord brought Isaiah 54: 4-17, to my heart and mind, a Scripture as the Great Physician He has used countless times in the past to minister to me; His words a salve upon my wounded heart:

4. 'Fear not, for thou shalt not be ashamed; neither be thou confounded; for thou shalt not be put to shame; for thou shalt forget the shame of thy youth, and shalt not remember the reproach of thy widowhood any more.

5. 'For thy Maker is Thy Husband; the Lord of hosts is His name; and thy Redeemer the Holy One of Israel; The God of the whole earth shall He be called.

6. 'For the Lord hath called thee as a woman forsaken and grieved in spirit, and a wife of youth, when thou wast refused, saith thy God.

7. 'For a small moment have I forsaken thee; but with great mercies will I gather thee.

8. 'In a little wrath I hid my face from thee for a moment; but with everlasting kindness will I have mercy on thee, saith the Lord thy Redeemer.

9. 'For this is as the waters of Noah unto Me: for as I have sworn that the waters of Noah should no more go over the earth; so I have sworn that I would not be wroth with thee, nor rebuke thee.

10. 'For the mountains shall depart, and the hills be removed; but my kindness shall not depart from thee,

neither shall the covenant of my peace be removed, saith the Lord that hath mercy on thee.

11. 'O thou afflicted, tossed with tempest, and not comforted, behold, I will lay thy stones with fair colours, and lay thy foundations with sapphires.

12. 'And I will make thy window of agates, and they gates of carbuncles, and all thy borders of pleasant stones.

13. 'And all thy children shall be taught of the Lord; and great shall be the peace of thy children.

14. 'In righteousness shalt thou be established; thou shalt be far from oppression; for thou shalt not fear; and from terror; for it shall not come near unto thee.

15. 'Behold, they shall surely gather together, but not by Me; whosoever shall gather together against thee shall fall for thy sake.

16. 'Behold, I have created the smith that bloweth the coals in the fire, and that bringeth forth an instrument for his work; and I have created the waster to destroy.

17. 'No weapon that is formed against thee shall prosper; and every tongue that shall rise against thee in judgment thou shalt condemn. This is the heritage of the servants of the Lord, and their righteousness is of Me, saith the Lord.'

If you have been the victim of domestic violence, you know all too well the shame, pain, and fear associated with that type of abuse. These words are for you as well; to call to your remembrance the Lord's desire to be your Husband and to minster to your deepest needs. Not only can He heal your wounds, He can fill you with peace as He delivers you out of all manner of fear. Jesus bore our shame, pain, and fear upon the cross. Remember, also, that, '…He was wounded for our transgressions: He was bruised for our iniquities, the chastisement of our peace was upon Him; and with His stripes, *we are healed.*' (Isaiah 53:5)

Chapter Ten:
Fear Is No Longer My Constant Bedfellow

The morning after a grand mal seizure was unsettling in all regards. I awoke exhausted and incontinent of urine. Walking was slow and difficult. My tongue was bitten, bleeding, or bruised; every muscle in my body was tender and sore; my head ached; my mind was foggy; the pit of my stomach was jarred; and my short-term memory was impacted. More than once, I fell to the floor from my bed during the seizure event; once having sustained a black eye as a result.

Although the physical injuries eventually healed, the memory effects appeared to have been permanent. In essence, certain facts and events were missing from my active memory and it was almost as though I needed to discover or learn them over again.

Since much of our personality is indeed shaped by the experiences we have had, I found myself somewhat inhibited and uncertain about particular events having occurred within the previous months. Occasionally, however, even the most vital essential information deeply-committed to memory and taken-for-granted eluded me. One particular low point was when I could not recall the exact date of my youngest son Jacob's December birthday. Mortified, ashamed, and with a broken heart, I had to bring myself to ask him. Fortunately, he was extremely understanding about the matter.

Few can imagine the fear associated with a seizure disorder. It was much more than merely the event itself, for that was only a very small aspect of it. During a seizure, I was not aware of what was occurring nor was I able to control it. It was not as though I experienced an attack of some sort, waited for it to pass, then gradually returned to a state of normalcy.

Rather, I experienced the episode on this vein:

I am being shaken, roused. The person is familiar; especially around the eyes, although I am not quite certain of his or her identity.

"Deb! Deb!" he is calling. It sounds like his voice is echoing down a vast tunnel. Eventually it normalizes. It is a male with dark hair. He begins speaking.

"You did it again," he informs me. "It happened again."

Confused, I wonder, *what is he talking about?* Suddenly, it dawns on me:

I don't...I don't know your name. Who are you?

It is as though I am slowly emerging from a deep fog. After a time, *I realize it's...my...husband...Matt.*

"Nnnnnnnnnoooooooooooooooooooo," I hear myself wail.

I have learned that there are some fears for which there are simply no adequate words. Exactly what are they? They are physical, psychological, biological, emotional, and cognitive. It was no overstatement to describe my fear in this way: **It was as though I felt terrified right down to my DNA.**

Perhaps first and foremost, there was the fear that a seizure might itself *occur.* Secondly, there was the worry surrounding the *damage* that a seizure might have caused to my memory or even to my brain. I was also concerned that seizure processes *themselves* might further harm my *body* as the convulsions, aspiration, loss of consciousness, and overall control robbed me of my ability to guard my bodily integrity; in addition, every physical pain, sensation, or symptom I felt was attributable to seizure aftereffects.

Beforehand, at least for me, there was also an impending foreboding associated with the threat of a seizure event. In fact, I found that the week prior to actually experiencing one, I had a bizarre, "otherworldly" sensation that often acted as a predictor of its occurrence—I have heard other individuals refer to their own such experiences as being an, "aura."

Next, I often had an immediate physiological dread of: falling asleep at night; losing my memories; becoming dependent upon my husband and family; of burdening, stressing or frightening them; or perhaps being unable to care for, provide for, or help to financially support them.

Worst of all, my memory was affected; the fear of losing my memories haunted me. Our memory is something very much taken for granted yet it forms the basis of all of our experiences; our knowledge base; as well as the wisdom we gave gained over the years. As I had soon begun to discover, it also shapes our personality. I found that not being able to recall facts, events, and other information had a chilling effect on both my behavior and actions. Afraid to do or say the wrong thing, I squelched many thoughts that came to me; those that I would have ordinarily acted upon. Much of my sense of self seemed to have been lost; my confidence seeping away as though through a gaping psychological wound. Admittedly, this lowered my self-esteem.

I studied a photograph of Matt and my five sons at a recent family celebration; a reunion of sorts. As much as I had wanted to be there with them that day, I'd declined to attend, concerned that I might have experienced a petit seizure event and placed the solemnity of the entire occasion in jeopardy. Although I realized my family might not have been able to fully comprehend this from my perspective, I much preferred to have been remembered as not having been present rather than having attended and experienced a possible seizure event (and subsequent critical lapse in memory) during that ceremony.

The fear that I experienced was often paralyzing. Countless times, I recalled the Lord's prophecy in my heart:

Fear not, for I have anointed you to be a witness as you have dreamed of; be bold in your confession.

It was a life ring during those times I was swept by fear and doubt.

The guilt of my having such a disorder was likewise overwhelming. I began and ended each day wracked with feelings of torment; as though I was bringing bitter consequences upon my children, husband, and family members. I felt intense guilt, shame, inadequacy, depression, and an abiding sense of blame and failure for having placed myself in a situation in which I became injured all those years ago.

This is not at all to indicate that the domestic violence I experienced was my fault, nor what other victims have suffered is a matter of blameworthiness; but that I had unwisely placed myself in a dangerous situation because I had walked away from the Lord's revealed will for my life. As a direct result, my son and I had both been physically and emotionally abused.

Several years ago, I had driven to another vacant, empty lot; this one on Seventh Avenue in the city of Troy which housed the dwelling within which I was once strangled and suffocated back in 1985. I had trouble remembering exactly which residence it was; nonetheless, I'd had a distinct, four-digit, black-and-white memory of the numeric address emblazoned into my mind for over twenty-five years, and drove there for several reasons; not the least of which was to prove to myself that I could indeed face the house of horrors from which Joshua and I had once prayerfully escaped.

As I slowly navigated that road, I searched my side view mirror. When I believed I had located the address, I pulled over and parked, reflecting back on my life. Yes, I realized there were no answers to be found lodged beneath that worn doormat; no key hidden there to unlock what had happened to Joshua and me so long ago. I then spent some time contemplating the life I had lived in the ensuing years since that attack, silently praying for strength.

I knew that whatever survived of that cobwebbed past no longer crept along that attic today; no ghosts of the past lurked in those shadows nor darkened that old doorway. Any terror that still haunted the chambers of my memory or horror that was locked away within my heart and mind *belonged solely to yesterday*. Would I now allow that murderous attempt to snuff my life out back then to define me *now* or shake my faith *today*? Wouldn't *that* have been the ultimate victimization—aside, of course, from my death itself—the consummate act of power and control?

I had learned well over the years that The Lord Himself held time in His very Hands. As the Alpha and Omega, He alone knew the end from the beginning; and only He had the power to prevent me from being denied the future He had intended for me all along. In fact, on 2/1/2010, exactly at sunrise, the Lord woke me from slumber and spoke these words in my heart:

It is time.

With that in my heart and mind, Matt and I attended Christian counseling with pastors from a local fellowship. After several meetings, the Lord opened my eyes. Finally, on Wednesday, 5/19/11, I spoke these long overdue words to my husband Matt: "I am sorry. I am very sorry for having been angry at you all these years. It wasn't your fault. I know it wasn't your fault. Please forgive me."

There was a tremendous amount of freedom in this revelation. In truth, to some extent, I hadn't forgiven him all these many years for his having rejected me back in the past when I had made known my feelings for him—in a sense, *I realized I had unfairly blamed Matt for the domestic violence I had suffered as well as the assault on me that had nearly taken my life and had resulted in my having had the seizures.* I had been blinded to that all this time—until the Lord revealed it to me. It was almost as though He had held up a spiritual mirror which enabled me to view that very ugly reality.

Early that June, Matt and I would report to Albany Medical Center for administration of a sleep-deprived EEG examination. In the neurology center, an electroencephalogram (EEG) measured the electrical activity of my brain during sleep while attached electrodes recorded and stored the changes that occurred in the normal pattern of that activity. I was told that the results would then be interpreted by a neurologist in the practice.

On the way home from that exam, Matt and I drove down New Scotland Avenue in Albany. Suddenly, I glanced up. Directly in front of us, at the very end of that street, was poised a *CVS Pharmacy*. For a time, I pondered what he and I had been through together during our 20-year marriage. It had been twenty-six years since he had hired me as a cashier and clerk to work in the *CVS Pharmacy* in downtown Troy. (In my view, that store had always represented much more than simply a fortuitous opportunity I had once availed myself of as a young, single mother; the Lord had truly used my time there--it had quite literally proven to have been the only prescription for my wounded, aching, heart.)

Later that week, the phone rang. Not surprisingly, I was told that the EEG examination I had undergone had indicated some irregularity in the electrical activity of my brain. Other than that, there was nothing definitive that could be explained to me; and a majority of the questions I posed concerning the results and what they meant went largely unanswered. I was again told that my only option was to take the medication I had been prescribed previously. When I inquired whether various other medications could prevent recurrent seizures; or if there were drugs for which the side effects could be controlled, I was again told that the neurologist, "was unable to assure me of any of that." I thanked the practice for the information and expressed my desire to obtain a second opinion.

Lord, please touch me and heal me, was the prayer of my heart.

As I had hung up from that phone call, I glanced up to my home library. My eyes fell upon an original copy of the book *Verdict on the Shroud*, by Kenneth Stevenson and Gary Habermas (1981). Beside it was a copy of *Report on the Shroud of Turin*, written by Dr. John Heller (1983), a member of the original *Shroud Research Team*; a book recently purchased for me by my son Caleb. I checked my email messages at that point, noting with significance that

I had just been the recipient of an email message from Barrie M. Schwortz, Editor and Founder of the *Shroud of Turin* Website (http://www.shroud.com/) and president of the *Shroud of Turin Education and Research Association, Inc. (STERA, Inc.),* a site to which I had begun to subscribe back when I had first learned to use a computer in the HVCC computer lab. Again, I marveled that the 1978 examination of the same cloth I had learned about in my Nana's home office decades ago still had forensic value and authenticity—even and especially now. Not only that, but the three-dimensional image on that cloth still cannot be replicated nor even *explained* by any known technology to this very day, in 2012.

Just as meaningful to me personally, I believe that the very same Lord Whose Body was once covered by that Shroud, still *heals* today—right up to this very moment. I am reminded of two additional Scriptures that speak to this very issue—Matthew 8:16-17, and I Peter 2:24, respectively:

When the even was come, they brought unto Him many that were possessed with devils; and he cast out the spirits with His word, and healed all that were sick; that is might be fulfilled which was spoken by Esaias the prophet saying, Himself took our infirmities, and bare our sicknesses.

Who His own self bare our sins in His own body on the tree, that we, being dead to sins, should live unto righteousness: by Whose stripes ye were healed.

I again sought prayer for healing while attending church services with my son Joshua and his girlfriend, Katie. After that meeting, a young man approached and sat down with me.

"I feel as though the Lord wanted me to tell you that Niacin prevents seizures," he conveyed. We talked for a few moments. While I knew that Niacin had health benefits, I was unaware it mitigated against seizures. Since that time, I have taken thousands of milligrams of Niacin (Vitamin B3) per day and the frequency and severity of seizures have greatly reduced. On prior occasions, I have had as many as ten seizures per week; but, according to my family, this past week, I am gratified to report that I only experienced one.

Just as meaningfully, as I sat in my home office and worked on this manuscript, I no longer had to *imagine* that I was a writer as I used to as a child--the Lord had truly fulfilled that dream and allowed me that very privilege over the past several years. As I typed on my laptop, I sipped a *7-Up®* soda, which had only recently been reintroduced and remarketed in the original classic 1970's version that I remembered so well. Turning to a display of photographs on my office wall, I studied a shot of my Uncle Jim and me from back in Christmas of 1964, in which I was perched upon his lap. Were he here, I wondered what my great uncle would think of the world of technology at my fingertips *today*, in 2012. As I contemplated that, it dawned on me that I had begun to purposefully nibble upon the end of a pencil.

At that moment, Matt came in and indicated that he planned on taking a trip to downtown Troy to run an errand. I knew that he would be driving right past Uncle Jim's old store on Fourth Street, and I asked my husband to take me through that neighborhood so I could see the old storefront. He agreed.

When we had pulled up and parked in front of what used to be the *Yett's News Room* in Troy, I was saddened that little remained of the original property—the brownstone store had been recently remodeled; the building was now covered by a new brick façade exterior. As we exited the car, I saw that even the sidewalk itself directly in front of the building had since been replaced--gone were the familiar cracks in the pavement that I had once known so well as a child—nonetheless, they are as cemented in my memory as the lines within the palm of my very own hand *today*. After all, it was there where I had once gleaned so many concrete life lessons from my Uncle Jim; and although neither he nor his home is any longer on this earth, those lessons have solidified and remained in my heart over time. For that, I will always be grateful. Matt and I lingered there for several moments; silently. Even for a writer...the right words somehow seemed to elude me.

Glancing up directly across the street to 174 Fourth Street, I now stood below in the very location where my uncle had often beckoned up to me as a child; while on the other side of that window pane on the third floor, I had frequently rapped upon that glass, calling down to him. Somehow, despite the circumstances, he had always responded to that call. The greatest lesson my uncle ever taught me was the reality of God's love. (For just a moment, I recalled the scent of *Lava®* soap; my strong and gritty uncle very much in my heart and on my mind. Warm feelings of happiness then began to wash all over me.) After a time, Matt and I turned and headed for home.

There was yet another visit I was constrained to make—this one down a seemingly more complicated road—I hadn't spoken to either of my parents in quite some time. While there were several underlying reasons for this, dwelling upon these would have been unwise. At the heart of the matter were issues of unforgiveness; I realized I still harbored resentment toward each of them due to events that had occurred long ago. This past week, I was able to meet with my mother and speak with her face-to-face for the first time in about six years. I shared my testimony with her and offered an opportunity for the two of us to begin to build a relationship from that point forward. I am happy to state that my offer was accepted; I trust that the Lord will direct my paths from here.

As I began to leave her home, something caught my eye. There, in her living room, was a six-drawer crème-colored veneer chest of drawers with brass knobs. I was floored!

"This can't be the same dresser that used to be in your bedroom back when I was little, can it?" I asked incredulously as I was inexplicably drawn to it.

"The one and the same," she assured me. "That's the original mirror also." I began toying with the brass knobs, beholding my image within that mirror for the first time in over forty-five years. I came to a realization--reflection upon one's past is normal and healthy; this, after all, is how we learn. However, undue rumination upon our pain, grief, and loss is *torment*; this brings suffering. In order to grow, we have to allow Him to heal those deeply-held wounds. He is the only One Who can see beyond our polish and veneer to truly open our heavy hearts.

What next might the Lord show me?

Today, I am on leave from law school as my healing and restoration by the Lord are very much works in progress. I have completed half of my law doctorate, but, unfortunately, due to the length of time of my leave—I have been notified that I may need to forfeit these earned credits and *reapply* for admission. Again, I pray that the Lord will restore what has been lost and strengthen me for what lies ahead— including any appeals process I may have to undergo with the NYS Bar Association. Regardless, I know I can rely upon the Lord for ultimate justice; it is the Holy Spirit Who first drew me toward law in the first place, and called me to advocate for victims of abuse, both in word and in deed.

Must I still be caught in the stranglehold of my past? No. With my husband Matt's love and support, as well as that of my five sons, the Lord has shown me that fear is no longer my constant bedfellow and I have been freed from the grip of domestic violence. Isn't it time then—for me to finally *break* free? Yes. I have it upon the very best authority of all—*it is time.*

About The Author

Deborah A. Tremblay lives, writes, and teaches from Watervliet, New York, with her husband and five sons. She considers it her objective to write, teach, counsel, and advocate in the area of therapeutic justice; to utilize the disciplines of law, mental health, addictions, and the social sciences to impact upon abuse issues in human behavior with emphasis on criminal justice, psychology, sociology, counseling, addictions, and, in particular, domestic violence.

Education

Juris Doctorate Candidate, Albany Law School of Union University, Albany, NY. Criminal Law Concentration; doctorate in progress.

MS in Mental Health & Substance Abuse Counseling, Nova Southeastern University's Fischler School of Education and Human Services Master of Science Program, Ft. Lauderdale, FL, June 2006. Completed 160-hour clinical internship at Continuing Treatment Services, an out-patient MICA facility operated by Samaritan Hospital, Troy, NY, Summer 2006.

MS in Criminal Justice, Specialty in Behavioral Sciences. Nova Southeastern University's Criminal Justice Institute Master of Science Program, Ft. Lauderdale, FL, September 2004.

BS in Criminal Justice Policy/Sociology, The Sage Colleges, Albany, NY. Honors in Criminal Justice, Magna Cum Laude. Member of Alpha Kappa Delta, International Honor Society of Sociology. May 2003.

AAS in Criminal Justice, Hudson Valley Community College, Troy, NY. High Honors in Criminal Justice. Member of Phi Theta Kappa, International Honor Society of the Two Year College. May 2000.

References

Bible references: Isaiah 53:5; Isaiah 54:4:17; Matthew 8:16-17; I Peter 2:24.

http://www.americanbar.org/content/dam/aba/migrated/domviol/docs/Domestic_Violence_Arrest_Policies_by_State_11_07.authcheckdam.pdf *Domestic Violence Arrest Policies by State. American Bar Association Commission on Domestic Violence. July 18, 2011.*

http://www.dviworld.org/ *Domestic Violence Institute.* July 17, 2011.

Family and Medical Leave Act of 1993.

http://www.lavasoap.com/products/lava-bar/ *Lava® Hand Soap* ("The Original Heavy-Duty Hand Cleaner"), 1893. July 18, 2011.

Looseleaf Law Publications, Inc. (2002). N. Y. C.P.L.R. 140.10(4). Arrest without a warrant; by police officer; when and where authorized in *Penal Law and criminal procedure law of the state of New York.* Flushing, New York: *Looseleaf Law Publications, Inc.*

http://www.mayoclinic.com *Mayo Clinic Website.* July 23, 2011.

NYS Strangulation Law, Model Penal Code. The Strangulation Prevention Act of 2010, enacted on November 11, 2010.

N.Y. Crim. Proc. Law § 140.10 (4)(C) NYS Mandatory Arrest Policy in Domestic Violence.

http://www.health.state.ny.us/ NYSDOH (2011). *New York State Department of Health Website.* July 17, 2011.

http://www.opdv.state.ny.us *Office for the Prevention of Domestic Violence,* noting that 44 percent of all women killed in the state in 2009 were killed as the result of domestic violence, and that women in abusive relationships who have been strangled by their abuser are 10 times more likely to be killed at some point. July 17, 2011.

http://shroud.com/library.htm *Shroud of Turin* Website. July 17, 2011.

Paoline, III, E.A. (2003). Taking stock: Toward a richer understanding of police culture. *Journal of Criminal Justice. 31,* 199–215.

Terrill, W. & Paoline, E.A., III & Manning, P.K. (2003). Police culture and coercion. *Criminology. 41,* 1003–1035.

Verdict on the Shroud, (1981). Based upon latest research, *Evidence for the Authenticity of the Shroud of Turin.* Stevenson, Kenneth E., and Habermas, R., Gary. Dell/ Banbury Books, Inc.

Violence Against Women Act (VAWA) of 1994. Reauthorized 2000, 2005, 2010.

Walker, L.E. (1979). *The Battered Woman.* New York: Harper & Row.

James Q. Wilson (1968). *Varieties of Police Behavior--The Management of Law and Order in Eight Communities.* Harvard University Press: Cambridge MA. Sixth Printing, 1976.

http://www.winthrop.org/departments/specialtycenters/
sleep-disorders-center/unusual-sleep-disorders.cfm
Winthrop University-Hospital Website. July 18, 2011.

http://www.7up.com 7-Up Soda ® "The Original Uncola."
July 18, 2011.

CPSIA information can be obtained
at www.ICGtesting.com
Printed in the USA
FFOW02n1054300414
5155FF